BEYOND
THE FOUR BLOCKS

Dearest Jimeke,

You are "Planted With Purpose!"
Your countenance is contagious.
You're brilliant, beautiful, and
wonderfully made in our Father's
Image. I'm so grateful to have
met you on my journey.
May the words forthcoming encourage
you to continue to pour into
God's people. Much love
Dr. Cornata

BEYOND
THE FOUR BLOCKS

A Memoir

Cernata C. Morse, PhD

Dr. C Speaks, LLC

FALLS CHURCH, VA

BEYOND THE FOUR BLOCKS

A Memoir

Copyright © 2019 by Cernata C. Morse, PhD

Cernata C. Morse, PhD /Dr. C Speaks, LLC
Falls Church VA 22041
www.drcspeaksllc.com/info@drcspeaksllc.com

Author's Note: I have tried to recreate events, locales and conversations from my memories of them. In order to maintain their anonymity in some instances I may have changed the names of individuals and places; in others I have changed identifying characteristics and details such as physical properties, occupations and locations.

Beyond The Four Blocks/ Cernata C. Morse, PhD -- 1st ed.
ISBN978-1-7332709-0-8

For my children – "The Morse Crew"

Zack II, Znada, & Zelexis each of you have been the heartbeats that kept my hope and dream alive for a *"Better Life"*.

Stand in your Purpose – Stand in your Power!

Reach for the moon, if you miss you'll be amongst the stars.
~Norman Vincent Peale

"For I know the plans I have for you," declares the Lord,
"plans to prosper you, not to harm you
plans to give you hope and a future."

JEREMIAH 29:11, NIV

Praise for Dr. Morse
and "Beyond The Four Blocks"

This book will resonate with so many who have suffered loss and are in the process of rebounding. A beacon of hope for those who have lost their voice and given up on their dreams, it's also an inspiration to help fulfill the dreams of others. A reminder that a foundation built on love, family and forgiveness, transcends all.

Dr. Walter R. McCollum, Higher Education Administrator.

~

I love this story. The language. The folks. The courage. How could I not? We start like this: *"My eyes open. The unmistakable odor of Mr. Clean spanks my nose. That's how I know it's Saturday. Scrubbed and rubbed to cloroxed perfection, our home is getting ready for Sunday. "* What in any other book would be a fine character, a protagonist, is here that unlikely creature of truth. A heroine. Charmed and damned in equal measure until her own resilient courage sets her free. Cernata. Dr. Morse. Well done.

Maggie White, Writer/Media Consultant

~

She had me from the first chapter, a sharply beautiful remembrance of childhood in a nearly forgotten corner of Alexandria, Virginia. In that time of hot summers and double-dutch, neighbors looked out for you, and generations built lives on faith and fine home cooking. When unexpected events force "Dr. C." to find her voice beyond her four blocks, we find it brave, ironic and never less than fascinating.

Dan Dalriada, Film/TV Professional

~

Cernata Morse has penned an engaging, open-hearted memoir filled with wisdom and hope. An accomplished scholar, teacher and businesswoman whose faith, family and friendships have sustained her through tragedy and desolation. Morse reflects deeply on her life's many crossroads, distilling from them bright gems of insight and inspiration for the reader.

Liz Netzel, Fresh Ink

DEAR READER

I invite you to experience a story of hard luck, hard times, and the hard work of forgiveness, all in hopes of the reward at the end of the road: To reconcile. To find my voice. To offer hope, even help.

There are no heroes or villains in this account, unless you can see them where I can't. Are they never what they first seem to be? Or is there a hero, and a villain, in each of us?

If you are intrigued by these questions, I welcome you as a companion on this journey—not yet complete—as I confront my life and the ways it was bent out of true, out of its intended shape, like a piece of fine wood in the hands of a bad carpenter. The culprit? Others' expectations. Like you, perhaps, I've spent my life trying to defy those expectations to shape the person I am meant to be.

With faith in God's impeccable timing, I'm still surprised at every twist and turn.

The road ahead beckons.

CHAPTER ONE

SATURDAYS

Late 60s, Early 70s, 409 Oronoco Street, Old Town, Alexandria, VA.
My eyes open. The unmistakable odor of Mr. Clean spanks my nose. That's how I know it's Saturday. Scrubbed and rubbed to cloroxed perfection, our home is getting ready for Sunday. The windows are opened to clear the air. My mother and grandmother are hanging fresh curtains washed the night before. No use trying to sleep as the sounds of grownups being busy scatter my hopeful little dream to bits. The sounds: vacuum cleaner humming, pots and pans moving around in the kitchen. And new smells of cooking. My grandmother's strong alto takes up a hymn until her voice dissolves into my mother's calling me to get up. "Rise and shine, we have work to do!" I do get up, put on jeans, tennis shoes and a shirt, then go downstairs to eat my cereal.

Dad's already gone to work.

My grandmother says, "I need you to go to Mr. Marty's."

I roll out my little pink bicycle with the white basket attached to the front handlebars. My grandmother has already made her list. I heard her on the phone with Mr. Marty earlier, telling jokes and explaining exactly how she wants her meat cut, saying I'd be around shortly to pick up everything.

And I'm wondering if I'm gonna be a good enough girl, am I going to get some candy? I'm pedaling along, passing folks saying, "Hey, Cernata, how you doin'?" Our projects take up four blocks. And I keep on rolling past, clinging my bell to let 'em know I'm coming. Now I'm powering up that last rise to Mr. Marty's. This is the steepest part, and I'm struggling because I'm a bit on the chunky side. But I am motivated. Up the hill I pump those pedals toward my reward. Candy. Maybe.

Maybe it won't happen today but if it doesn't? Surely next time.

I arrive at Mr. Marty's, park my bike and bounce through the door.

"You came to pick up Ms. Dot's order?"

"Yes sir," I say, as always, because I've been raised to say "ma'am" and "sir" to my elders. Mrs. Marty walks down long rows of groceries, canned and dry goods stacked on shelves, filling my list, while Mr. Marty leans over his butcher block counter cutting the meat (exactly as instructed). He wraps it in salmon brown paper, and tapes it securely to fit in the basket of my bicycle with all the other groceries Mrs. Marty has just brought to the front of the store.

Meanwhile, my eyes have memorized the candy section. Rows and rows of Bee Bee Bats, JuJu Bees and the Sugar Stripes my grandmother loves. Mrs. Marty, standing near the cash register, says, "Cernata, come here." And when I come up to her, she has a little brown paper bag to give me.

"You go fill up this bag."

"But I don't have any money."

"You're one of the good kids." And she drops a quarter in the cash register.

"It's paid for. Get the candy, and I'll call Catherine." Because I am terrified that my mother will think that I'd *asked* for the candy. I wanted the candy, but I imagine how the conversation will go when I get home:

"Look, look, I got this candy!"

"Did you ask for that?"

"Oh, no!"

I pay for the groceries from the envelope my grandmother has given me. Mrs. Marty makes change and puts it back in the envelope. I savor the moment, the growing up. My grandmother has trusted me with the money. And my parents have trusted me to make this journey beyond the four blocks.

Coming back, it's downhill all the way. The air whips around me. I've got the weight of the groceries in the basket, but I'm managing. I zoom past a friend who shouts, "Hey, you wanna play jacks with me?" Further along, someone suggests double-dutch.

"In the alley?" Because there are alleys winding all through our project.

"When I get back!" I say, because I'm good at double-dutch.

At home, some of Sunday's meal is nearly done. They've cleaned and parched the vegetables, prepped the meat and set it aside to rest. Bread is rising under a clean linen cloth. There's a dress or two hanging up; the ironing board is folded and tucked out of sight. My entire church outfit is laid out in the bedroom I share with my grandmother and nieces. There's a dress hanging from a thread somewhere in the room. And my little patent leather shoes are polished and placed on the floor, side by side. I'll be wearing white socks because it's summer. A girl always wears a slip...but now I am asking can I go back outside to play?

A bunch of us kids gather until noon. Double-dutch jump rope is the thing. Everybody's in the alley and we're jumping up a storm. Two ropes swing in crisscrossing arcs, touching the sky, touching the ground, the sky, the ground. Players move in and out, feet drumming the pavement in near-military precision. Our mastery is evident. Spectators are awed. Among the spectators, one of my nieces dares to complain that she never gets to double-dutch because I am always in the middle of it. I yell back, "You're too young and don't know how to jump in, just stand back and watch!"

~

Noon rolls around. We abandon our street games and go home. Once we enter the house the begging starts: "Could you *please,* cut the television on?" Because...

It's "SOUL TRAIN"! There is one TV in the house, and there on its black and white screen is the train, jamming toward us. Don Cornelius is onscreen, and we're in the living room, glued to the TV, trying to figure out, "What's the latest dance!" Trying to get those moves down, my nieces and I gauge every nuance of the week's new dances. The minute the show is over, we run out of the house and onto the sidewalk to practice what we've learned. Singing, dancing, posing, we are unfettered joy.

I come back inside to find my mother poised to do my hair, pressing iron and curlers heated and ready. We will be turning my long hair into a truly magnificent display of Shirley Temple ringlets. I have a LOT of hair.

The clickety click of the curlers.

The "My Knight" hair grease.

"Mom, can I wear my hair out?"

But we both know it will never do to leave this hair untamed. Left on its own, it will curl itself into knots. I sit patiently, squeaking out only once, "Mom, you're burning me!" as the hiss of steam veers close when she pulls out a curl. At last finished, she ties up my curls to keep Shirley Temple in place. This creation must last until tomorrow.

Then I take my bath.

~

Night falls, everybody's in bed, and my mom is watching "Perry Mason". My grandmother sits nearby in her little chair, praying over the house, praying over us all. My dad may or may not be there. He might be hanging out, doing his thing, meaning to come back later. My mom will sit up and wait for him and it might be late, but no matter, this is her quiet time. Oftentimes, Perry winds up looking at her instead of her looking at him, as she, so gently, falls asleep.

~

Next morning, is that a rooster crowing outside our windows or am I still dreaming? We're on high alert; the household snaps to attention. My grandmother's feet hit the floor. Covers are whipped off beds. Children are rousted out. It is time to go to God's house.

We smell biscuits baking. Lord have mercy. And her coffee. Though I don't drink it to this day, I love the smell of that fresh-perked coffee. It is my grandmother's drink: black, no cream. After breakfast of bacon, eggs and biscuits—all of us sitting around one small table—out the door we go.

We are perfectly dressed, immaculate. My handsome father, if he's going, is suited and booted attractively. My mom shines from head to toe, crowned with a hat. Momma Dot, our grandmother, is similarly glorious in hat, gloves, hose, and pumps. We get in the car and head to Ebenezer Baptist Church.

~

From the time we arrive we're busy, that is, from Sunday School until church lets out around 1 or 1:30. Kids are now running around playing. Grownups are relaxing outside the church talking or making plans to get together for mid-day dinner at someone's house. It is the time of potlucks, all put together by community hands. Somebody might say, "Well I can have the choir over. Bring some dishes, and I'll prepare the meat."

And isn't that the best in the world? Because not only do we get our family's home cooking, but everybody else's. Everybody else who can cook, that is. (We've already figured out who can't, so we can politely decline.)

A store called "Miss Blue's" is at the corner at the end of the block from our church. Miss Blue has the best, big ol' ice cream sandwiches. You can choose vanilla or Napoleon (vanilla, chocolate and strawberry arranged in precise blocks). And they only cost a quarter, which we can afford because we have budgeted. (Not all of our stash goes in the collection plate.) We hold a little back because Miss Blue has penny candy and soda pop for sale along with the ice cream sandwiches.

"Oh, y'all been to Miss Blue's." Our parents finally notice we are back among them.

"Uh, yeah."

"Get in the car."

And so we go home, take off our church clothes, put on something casual, and most likely, sit down for dinner.

Tomorrow is Monday. Time to prep for school.

CHAPTER TWO

A CAST OF CHARACTERS

I imagine them sitting along both sides of a long table, each holding the script of my life, as if ready to step on stage and play their part.

LILLIAN DOROTHEA JONES-WEBB, "MS. DOT"

When I think about the characters who shaped my life, she is the first person who steps up. My grandmother was a preacher's kid. I witnessed her, every day, being grounded in faith. Always praying, always giving, and always sacrificing. I saw that through my whole life with her. Beautiful in the flesh, petite and shapely, she had a smile that would permeate a room.

She loved her father, Reverend John L. Jones. She talked to me about living in a time when inter-racial marriages were not welcome. My great-grandmother married an African-American man, Reverend Jones, down in Charlottesville, Virginia. She was cast out of her family for that choice, because they were passing as Caucasian. But my grandmother dearly loved this good man, her father, and passed on to me the principle of loving people not for the color of their skin but for the content of their heart—and, of course, their character. "You're going to be judged by the color of your skin, but don't you judge people by the color of *their* skin," she said to me once. And then touched her heart. I remember that just like it was yesterday. As I've learned more about my genealogy, I've found we are many shades of brown. Through it all, my parents looked for a better day, when those many shades of brown would be fully accepted.

Ms. Dot was a woman who sacrificed for her family. My mother was her only child, but she sacrificed for all those around her. When her nephews went off to war, packages and letters followed them. She was a strong matriarch in her family, little as she was. Petite, adorable, this tiny jokester was loved by all, including taxi drivers and bus drivers—which was a good thing, since she never drove.

MR. WEBB, THE MAN WHO WALKED AWAY

According to the story my grandmother told me about her husband (that would also be the story that went around the neighborhood) "he had walked away" when my mother was about five. He came home one day, showered, ate, did his chores, sat down to dinner with the whole family, played a little bit with his child, and then turned to my grandmother and said: "I'll see you soon." He walked out the gate, down the road, and disappeared with nothing but the clothes on his back.

As a result, my grandmother's family now centered around my mother and her father, Reverend Jones, who had already been living with them since it had become obvious he'd need care as he aged. My grandmother would always there for her father. She was the third oldest of seven children (the middle child), which might explain her devotion to others. As for the husband who walked away, my grandmother would never talk about him or what he'd done. She never mentioned him, *that man*, Mr. Webb. She went silent on the subject of "the man who walked away".

My grandmother was born in 1896. My mother in 1920. And I grew up in the era when whatever happened in the home stayed there. Bedroom discussions and quarrels were private. Kids had no place in them. In that household, my mother grew up as the peacemaker, and very much the protector—she became the foundation of our home.

CATHERINE VALDORISE WEBB-STANTON, MY MOTHER

She was tall, and absolutely drop-dead gorgeous. Everyone knew her either as "Miss Catherine," or "Mama Catherine." Now, my grandmother was jovial. She would crack jokes and keep you laughing, but my mother had a quiet nature. Since she was raised by her grandfather, Reverend Jones, you could say that she too was a preacher's kid. In that atmosphere, my foundation for knowing God came easy: I was born into it. On my dad's side, there were uncles upon uncles—all ministers. There was no way of *not* knowing God in my life. I went to school, but my social life was soaked up by church. We were in the youth choir, Sunday School, The Sunshine Band, and Junior Ushers. My whole life was church.

And every Sunday we entered the church and walked proudly to our seats. Because we were well-dressed and eager to show off the work of our mother's hands. It was undeniable: my mother had a knack for fashion. Though she was sent by Reverend Jones to study fashion in New York City, her heart was back in Charlottesville, with her family and soon-to-be husband. When she left school and returned home, she gave up her formal pursuit of fashion, though she never lost her love of it nor her creative knack. My mom put everything she learned in New York to work for her family and others: making dresses for kids at Easter and other holidays, especially for those who didn't have as much as we did, little as that was.

My mother and my grandmother were dress designers and seamstresses for some of Alexandria's most prominent women, including lawyers' wives, judges' wives and other women who were judges themselves. Mama's taste was classic; it reminded me of the movies' great costume designers, who built clothes for the likes of Katherine Hepburn, Audrey Hepburn and Lauren Bacall. That style seeped into me. (Somewhere in a past life I must have moved to the beat of the Harlem Renaissance, lindy hopping at The Savoy Ballroom.)

During the day my talented mother and grandmother worked cleaning houses or as companions for prominent Alexandria families like the Ayers. At night, they sewed. My sister and I were often among the best dressed women not just in church, but the whole town. Just like our grandmother and mother. Class and style were celebrated in our household. We even had a brand-new Wurlitzer piano.

~

My mom would get brown bags from the grocery store. She would bake a lot of bread and make soup. Then she'd fill her brown bags with bread and plastic containers with soup and take them to the men hanging out next to the corner market. We called them hobos back then. But they were just like today's homeless. My dad would be reading the paper, which he was fond of doing, and see her get ready to leave.

"Where you going?"

"I'm going down to the corner store."

"O.K., just be careful."

And she'd go down and hand out the food, including the jam my grandmother stuck in at the last minute.

I seem to remember that at Christmas my mom would sneak a piece of meat in each bag as well. But especially when it got cold, she would make her soup for the men next to the corner market standing around a big trash where they had made a fire to keep warm.

When they integrated the schools, and the weather was bad, my mother would pull out her big ol' tanker of a car, grab up a bunch of us neighborhood kids and trolley us across town to school.

Because that's what community did back then.

LUCIAN WILLIS STANTON... MY FATHER, THE COUNTRY BOY

He was a fast runner. No one could catch him once he decided not to be caught. Quite curious about the natural world around him, his love of animals was abiding. Long, lean and fleet of foot, he could often be glimpsed skirting through the woods, across the fields and beyond. Was he running *to* something or *from* something? It was never easy to tell. To call out his talent for speedy escapes from the possibility of scolding, capture, or other forms of bother, his family nicknamed him "Peter Rabbit." Over time it became, "Mr. Pete."

He was the youngest boy of a family of fifteen siblings. Five brothers, the rest females. And you want to talk about dominant? His sisters were bold, outspoken women. (Which may explain where I get my nature. My mother would sometimes say, "Is that *my* daughter?") Indeed, my outspoken, determined character settled in early.

Once grown up and married, Dad was hard-working in a variety of trades. As a butcher, he could bring home good cuts of meat with the blessing of his employers. Working in a tire shop, he might be called on to change the massive tires of tractor-trailers, since he was the only one trusted to do it. In one of the stories passed down, there was mention of an incident in the garage. The owner had a rifle and my father was cleaning it when a round left in the chamber went off and caused the accident that cost him his eye. (He spent the rest of his life with a glass replacement.)

But I can see, looking back, that he was enabled…he didn't learn early on that actions have consequences. After all, he was the baby of all those females. (His mother died when he was around 16. And he married when he was 17.) So, there were always excuses for everything he did that didn't turn out quite right. He was a *very* attractive country boy ready to charm his way around any issue. No surprise that when he came to the city, he was buck-wild. Always well-groomed… but hanging in the wrong circles.

Still, during that time, my mother would never allow anyone to question his actions. In our household, we respected our elders. Besides, my father was always a provider in our family; we had to respect his position as the head of the household no matter what was going on.

I am sad never to have met my father's parents, particularly his mother, after whom I am named: Cernata, or Znada, the warrior.

(Census documents from the time show my grandmother signing her name both ways: "Znada" and "Cernata").

KENNETH WILLIS STANTON, THE BROTHER I NEVER SAW

In the early 1940s my parents were a young, newly married, couple. They'd left Charlottesville for Alexandria where they would have a better chance of finding work. My mother was light-skinned enough to pass for Caucasian. When she went into labor with her first child, it turned into an emergency. My dad rushed her to Alexandria Hospital, the nearest to their home, where she was admitted. The staff took her for "white." At that particular time in our universe they labeled all our people "colored," no matter the variation in hue. Once they took notice of my father, tall and handsome though he was, with silky hair and high cheek bones, something made them ask if he was colored. Not willing to lie, he said yes. Once they knew who *he* was, they knew who *she* was.

My brother was born. My father said he was healthy. Only when he arrived the next day for a visit, did he hear the news. Their son had died. Mysteriously. The staff said that the baby had died of pneumonia, with no further details offered as they rushed my father out of the hospital with my mother.

Two years later, she gave birth to my older sister in 1946 in our little house in Old Town Alexandria. She had no desire to return to that hospital.

About 13 years later, I was born in Washington, D. C., up the road from Alexandria.

MY SISTER, VALDORISE MONTEZE STANTON

She was gorgeous, Lena-Horne-gorgeous, a straight-A student and musical genius; I mean, she was just brilliant on that Wurlitzer piano. My family worked themselves into the ground to make sure she was able to go to college. So I grew up in a family with all kinds of talent. And, I'll admit, I did have my share. In church, I learned the art of public speaking at a young age. I learned to read people; I could look past the exterior to see their truth, who they really were.

But with my sister up ahead of me, I always aspired to be like her, though I wasn't the straight-A student…and, in my mind, I wasn't drop-dead gorgeous. I was on the heavier side, the chunky daughter, the chubby one, the one with a sister who was tall and lean and lovely. You can imagine how I felt. Still, my parents would encourage me: "Cernata you can do it, you can do anything." And I don't think they meant any harm, but all the while they were shaping my expectations with *their* expectations of who I should be. They would hint, "your sister gets straight As, your sister plays the clarinet, the oboe and the bassoon."

Of course I obliged them and picked up the oboe and the alto and bass clarinet (though with mixed results). I didn't like the oboe, loved the clarinet, and even tried the piano, but didn't keep it up. I did master the clarinet, alto and bass since being part of the orchestra and band felt natural. So, I had my share of musical gifts, for one a strong voice and a secret ambition to sing R & B. Truth be told, all of us loved music. I can still hear Aretha Franklin's voice trailing out the bedroom as my sister played her 45s on Saturdays. Oh, my yes, we were all subjects of the Queen of Soul. We caught on to that genius early.

But I couldn't get the straight As. I just wasn't that student.

MOM LOUISE, MY MOTHER'S BEST FRIEND FOREVER

Mom Louise claimed her perch in our family early on. We all met her when she came to Alexandria from Mooresville, NC. Truly a Southern girl, she fell into that special category of phenomenal Southern cooks whom anyone feels blessed to know, especially when you're waiting to be served up a plate. She was a widow and had lost her only son to a tragic death. But know this and you'll know everything about Mom Louise and my mom—they were best friends forever. But the funny thing was that Mom Louise was in most ways the opposite of my mother. This short, stout, dark and sassy woman spoke her mind and enabled *nobody*. I soon learned in my teenage years that she had been abused as a teenager and, generally, had experienced a life of extreme hardship. But she had a very loving heart for my mother who relaxed and laughed easily in her company. Their special friendship allowed Mom Louise to point out things my mother was doing to enable our family throughout its bumpy history of mistake upon misjudgment. My mother would listen carefully, but her heart couldn't stop itself. It was so big! All she would say was "I know Louise! I know…"

And Mom Louise loved my grandmother, "Mama Dot", to pieces. Mom Louise would always cook her favorite foods, including her incomparable pound cake, and make certain she had a pot of fresh perked coffee available whenever we visited. At every crucial point in my life, she would turn up, an angel, heaven sent.

CHAPTER THREE

THE MAP OF MY HEART

OLD TOWN, ALEXANDRIA. When I think of my hometown, in the 60s, I remember it in summer. Back then Alexandria was a very small town sitting just outside Washington, D. C. where we enjoyed life in a true neighborhood. I knew the owners of Timberman's Drug, the Dart Drug Store, and G. C. Murphy's. I remember when they built the brand-new courthouse. And playing in its "pool." Call it that if you will. (I'm chuckling at the memory.) They'd put a fountain in front of it. We inner city kids didn't have any other kind of pool—unless you count the fire hydrants some kids would open up for a blast of water when the temperature rose and the humidity would smack you flat. So we would just sneak down to the courthouse and stick our feet in the water. Of course we would always get chased out. Seems funny looking back. Just little kids wanting to cool their feet, and not giving up.

THE BERG. Growing up in the 60s and 70s our neighborhood was more like one big family. The mothers looked out for each other's children, and no child would ever stray one block without someone looking out a window, or standing in the door—with a wave, or a "hello," or, "how's Miss Catherine?". Just checking in to make sure we were safe. Those were our lives as kids. Being part of a family, part of a neighborhood, just being happy playing outside together. Of course, there was one thing you had to pay attention to: *"Don't let the streetlights come on, and you're not in the house!"*. If I heard my mother calling down the block, "Cer-na-ta!" drawn out just like that, I knew I was in trouble. And it was impossible not to hear her, because it was so quiet back then. She would go right to the same spot every time to call me. She knew I would know her voice, because we each knew our mother's voice, like little sheep gone astray, waiting to be called back to the fold.

Also available to bring home the occasional wanderer was the town sheriff, familiar to us all, the one who could be counted on to bring home a man who'd drunk too much. Along with his car. In our neighborhood people took care of each other, in ways dating back to its founding during the Civil War, when "The Berg" was whispered about as a sanctuary for black refugees fleeing The South. These fugitives would join Free Blacks already settled in communities like The Bottoms and Hayti. They would look for work with the military, on the wharfs, the railroads or in encampments where they built barracks for soldiers and destitute freedmen. "The Berg" was named for the particular group of fugitive black people who fled Petersburg, Virginia to settle in northeast Alexandria after Union troops occupied it in 1861.

In 1945, public housing was built in The Berg; the hundred-some units would cover several blocks of Old Town. Sure enough, it was a "housing project" named for Samuel Madden, the first African-American pastor of the Alfred Street Baptist Church.

Over time, the history of the community and its roots faded, though it remained tightly knit, as befitted a place first established as a sanctuary. The curious can discover its too-little known history online with the Virginia Foundation for the Humanities, or make a visit to Alexandria's Black History Museum, which I recommend.

I'm proud of my roots in The Berg. It was the foundation for many a prominent citizen. One in particular was Alexandria's longest serving mayor former Mayor William D. Euille. In the 50s, 60s and 70s it was a community with up-and-coming African-Americans who branched out to surrounding white communities and purchased homes, slowly transforming the landscape of the city. Which in turn caused the resistance to integration of public schools in the early 70s, recalled in the film, *Remember the Titans.* In the film, "The Berg" was used as shorthand for "the ghetto," a hard word for me to recall and accept. Now, though my hometown is a reflection of pain unrecognized from the past, my younger self remembers The Berg simply as home, a pinpoint on the map of my heart. I cherish the memory of that time and place where everyone within a mile's radius knew their neighbors. My Alexandria was a small, segregated, community. But as a young child I wasn't always aware of its boundaries. Washington D. C. offered a different twist.

GARFINCKEL'S. Two blocks from the White House, the old Garfinckel's department store also has a place in my heart. Its flagship store was not particularly welcoming to "colored people" in the early 60s, nor did it allow us to try on clothes. Why is it on the list then, of places in my heart?

This.

I hold a memory of my mother and grandmother, after a full day's work outside the home. It's night; they're sewing...

My mother could create patterns out of pieces of newspaper. She was inspired by the clothes shown on mannequins she would see in department stores—the same stores where she was not allowed to enter through the front door. Like Woodward & Lothrop. And Garfinckel's. I remember my dad taking my mom and me over to Garfinckel's...off of 14th and F Streets in D.C. My mother was always immaculately dressed. But my father would be livid, saying, "Why do you need to do this!" My mom would simply say, "I need to see the latest fashions to make a dress for one of my clients." I remember she kept a little notepad in her pocket, and her purse always had a little money in it—enough to make a purchase to buy us time in the store. I would be all dressed up as we made our way in through the back door, *for colored only.* And my mother would find a design she liked on one of the mannequins. I remember her sketching very quickly, and then she would buy something small, like a handkerchief, before we hurried out of the store.

But I also remember, as a little girl, standing in that store, with people just watching us, just *watching* us. I sensed my mother was hurrying, like she was not welcome. And I kept thinking, if you're not welcome, why are you here? Right? I would ask, "Why are we going to *this* store?" And she would say, "Cernata, you don't understand, just don't say anything." I was always asking questions. I was inquisitive. I was a kid.

Garfinckel's was where my mother shined as a designer, though the memory is, of course, bittersweet. (And, in fairness to the now defunct Garfinckel's: by the 70s they were employing a somewhat diverse workforce and showing mannequins in different skin tones. Still, its reputation may have contributed to its demise, since affluent African-Americans tended to shop elsewhere.)

But that's how we made it, my mom, my dad, my grandmother, our whole knuckling-down family. We stood up straight, and got on with life. I look around now and see society, and I think, according to the data, to the demographics, we were considered poor. But I didn't know I was supposed to be poor, because I was one of the best dressed children at church, at school. Anywhere. I would grow to be nearly six-feet tall. When I stepped out, I stepped out boldly. Which is not to say I didn't, from time to time, get knocked down.

THE AYERS' HOUSE. Mr. and Mrs. Ayers were among Alexandria's prominent citizens. Her mom was elderly, in failing health. Mom would go clean the house and help out. I would sometimes go with her on the days we didn't have school. I'd settle in a downstairs room to do my homework. Then, I'd hear Mrs. Ayers talking to my mom.

"Catherine, is Cernata downstairs?"

"Yes, ma'am, they didn't have school today. She's fine, she's doing her homework."

Then Ms. Ayers would say, "Well tell her to come on upstairs. I want her to sit with me."

It was lunchtime, and she would make, maybe, a grilled cheese sandwich and tomato soup. When I look at works like, *The Help*, while I believe the truth of that particular story, I also knew that the people my mom worked for were different. They didn't treat her as if she was "less than." They knew my birthday and celebrated holidays by making up a big basket for my mom. There would be a gift envelope with cash in it; there would be all sorts of food items in the basket, fruits, nuts, maybe a turkey or some other meat to make a special dinner. They also knew my mom baked so there would be sugar and flour, every item on a baker's shopping list. I remember that family fondly, not just for the gifts, but their kind regard for us all. For Easter, they knew my mom liked lilies, so they would send her one in the florist's delivery truck. My father was blessed too. For a while, he worked for a butcher and seafood provisioner in Alexandria: on holidays they too would send him home with packages. We lived in the projects, but we got deliveries!

My parents drew people to them. It was their character; their vibe, they were good people, and they put it out there.

THE MARKETS. You've met Mr. and Mrs. Marty, the family who lived above the grocery and welcomed our business and my visits on the little pink bicycle. Although I might bring the needed amount of cash, placed in an envelope by my grandmother, at Mr. Marty's you could also pay, as the old folks say, "on time." Another family, the Santullos, ran a market on the other side of town. Right there on Duke Street, right by one of the first African-American churches, Shiloh Baptist. They had everything you could imagine: fresh greens and the whole body of animals destined for the table. Tongue, tripe. Every part of the cow from the end to the beginning; every part of the pig from the rooter to the tooter! People from the South loved this particular market, but everybody gathered there, especially around holidays, because you could get anything you'd need for your special meal. And the greens were fresh, *everything* was fresh off trucks rolling in from North Carolina and Southern Virginia, heaped high with the wonder of small farm vegetables...including the turnips my father loved.

A & P, with the "green stamps", was the first chain store to arrive in the 60s, putting Mr. Marty's, and later Santullo's, out of business. Mom would collect those green stamps and save up for a nice piece of dinner wear to dress her table. She would put together her little list—never straying from it—while she shopped at these stores, paying cash.

EBENEZER BAPTIST CHURCH. The majority of our neighbors in The Berg were African-Americans whose lives centered on a strong sense of community with the church as our foundation. (I counted once; there were at least seven churches of various denominations in our neighborhood.) Our family belonged to Ebenezer Baptist Church, at 909 Queen Street. I remember being at church almost every night during the week. Our whole family was involved in the music ministry, building fund, prayer meetings, ushers, and more. You name it, we were in it, involved in every activity of that church.

As I mentioned earlier, it was the church that gave me the chance to master the art of public speaking and performing on stage. You've heard that my sister was phenomenally talented in music, and that I attempted to follow in her footsteps. You may also remember that I did play the clarinet and was blessed to have a voice to sing, but I never mastered that piano. Though my sister and I shared a gift for music, and I would stay involved in music ministry all my life, I needed to find my own niche. Thankfully I did: the stage. As I look back, being a "natural" on stage was something I took for granted without giving it a name, much less attaching purpose to it. That would come later. And isn't it interesting when we hit that moment of epiphany and realize that a special gift—the one that can move your forward—was there all along?

Once I had my own family, they too were involved in Ebenezer Baptist. My soon-to-be husband and I were married in that church. All three of our children were baptized there and as they grew, became involved in youth ministry, Sunday School, music ministry and just about everything else. This was their childhood too!

I've come to terms with life in my first church, and what I truly know is this: my foundation of Christian knowledge and understanding couldn't save me or my children from the trials of our lives to come, but it did give us a sense of balance to weather its storms.

T. C. WILLIAMS HIGH SCHOOL. Remember "The Titans?" I do, every time I go back for class reunions and meet up with my fellow Titans at "T.C". The high school has a long and storied history, particularly during the year it first integrated, and first merged with two other schools to build a championship football team. Thus, the movie. But for me, it was the place I returned to graduate after some lost years away. And though it now offers the gamut of educational options for a highly diverse population, in my time there I was encouraged by a counselor to seek out a work training program. Higher education was not mentioned. But no worries; I just kept moving from the bottom up, as you'll see.

ESMONT. My early childhood memories of our family include traveling to visit my mother and grandmother's family in the suburbs of Charlottesville, VA. Those visits, especially to the family's church in the little town of Esmont, remain some of the most enjoyable moments in my life. Every August, we would go down for their "homecoming," a joyous celebration. And though the drive down did seem like it took forever, the fun started the moment we got there. My nieces and I would play games, sing, and explore the neighborhood, not knowing that our visits would become a storehouse of memories that would feed us throughout our lives. None of us knew in the moment, how we would come to cherish those times! We couldn't have known then that sitting around the table in fellowship with friends and family was giving us the stuff of life itself! Those times would settle into our hearts and mind, keeping us attached to the idea that life can be good—and is meant to be just that. Visiting "the country" was the epitome of our family life.

And oh, my goodness, the food! There was *some* cooking goin' on in that house!

But our family had always poured our hearts into cooking. The aromas told us we were home the minute we stepped through the door of our little house in The Berg. The smell of baked bread. The steamy sweetness of fresh-made jams. I can remember the rustle of paper bags as my grandmother packaged up gifts for our guests. And it worked both ways. Those that gave, received! When we travelled to Charlottesville to visit family, my sweet great Aunt Muriel would say, "Dorothy, I did all my jams!" and they would load up our car with those fresh jams and preserves, and fresh vegetables put up in Mason jars. Beets and green beans and turnips…of course. Then my great uncle John would go out to the smokehouse and get the ham he had cured for my mother since she was special to them as an only child. "Catherine, I've cut a ham for you!" And he would load it in the back of the car for her. He knew that my dad loved ham too. So, my mom would always have a ham and a turkey for the holidays.

The same held true when we went to visit with my dad's five sisters, who'd moved north from Buckingham, Virginia. These strong women embraced life fully, and were braced in turn by the occasional toddy. Toe-to-toe they would stand with any drinking man without a hint of swaying off-kilter. But they were careful. At the end of a day of celebration, and perhaps one toddy too many, they would say, "Y'all are stayin' here for the night, we're beddin' everybody down."

It was a great time, peppered with non-stop laughter, fun and talking, loud and all at the same time, around the dinner table. And, oh, yes, we never missed a chance to look around that table and remark upon what a fine-looking family we were. You may smile, but great looks ran on both sides of my family! It was a theme, you might say, along with the ongoing need to bring our fine selves together around a well-laid table.

These are memories from the map of my heart…a dear old patchwork quilt of warm places to wrap me in comfort when I need it.

CHAPTER FOUR

1972

My mom died when I was 12, soon to turn 13.

The phone call came in from members of the church. They'd been called by an eyewitness who knew my parents.

Back then, not everyone had a phone in their home, but there was usually at least one per apartment building, and, within Alexandria's tight-knit community, there was always a way to make sure an urgent message got where it needed to go. We got the call, we rushed to the hospital. My father was roughed up, but he was deeply concerned about my mother.

She was in bad shape.

They were going to Baltimore to attend a memorial service in honor of my late Aunt Lois. She was a social activist (seems to run in the family) and her dream of building a soup kitchen had become a reality. As they proceeded south on Route 1 at the intersection of Henry and Duke Streets in Alexandria, the car was t-boned by a teen-age drunk driver running a red light. As my father wrestled with the steering wheel to steady the car and keep it from flipping over, my mother was tossed all around the interior, her body colliding with one solid surface after another. At the hospital they'd done x-rays, kept her for three days, said everything was fine and sent her home. But there were, after all, complications.

That weekend after my mother was discharged from the hospital, she went into crisis. Her stomach started to bloat, like she was pregnant. Her skin started to wash out. Lord, it was so pale.

Before the crisis hit, I'd been away for the day, having been given permission to attend a wedding with a friend. When they dropped me back, I remember walking down the street toward our house and seeing it all lit up, every light in the house on. That was not normal. And I started running. I saw a car from New York parked near the house. My relatives. I got to the top of the stairs to encounter my father who was panicked, "Your mother is deathly ill, and you're not here!" The house was full of family, all upset.

Once I was up the stairs, my mom grabbed my hand, "OH, Cernata, I am so sick." I said, "Mom, lean on me," because I was a big girl. I had just finished walking her to her chair when she burst out, "Get me back up, get me to the bathroom!" I got her to the bathroom and she vomited black blood everywhere. An ambulance came flying in…they took her off…and she never came back home. Her spleen had ruptured in the accident and she was bleeding internally. Nobody had diagnosed it at the time, though once she returned to the hospital the spleen was finally removed.

In the hospital for a second time, she got better! She could walk down to the nurses' station. She would walk with me to the end of the corridor, and then watch out the window as I went to get my lunch every day. I'd say, "Don't worry ma, I'll be right back." And she'd say, "Don't hurry, I'll be here when you do."

But I saw it coming. One day, she took a turn for the worse. A staph infection had taken hold and couldn't be beaten. Medical malpractice? Later, I asked my dad, "Why didn't you do something?" I was furious. But back then? He reminded me that we were "colored people"; we didn't question anything.

For my mom's month-long stay in Alexandria hospital, I was there. I went every day, remembering it was where my brother had died as a newborn in 1944. The staff allowed me to come in through the back door, up the staircase, walk down the hall and then slip into her room. Since I was a big girl, they took me for older, sixteen rather than not quite thirteen.

The nurses told my father, "This young lady is the best we've ever seen, she takes the best care of her mom." I would run down the hall and get her things; I would get water for the lady who was her roommate. I was no problem. I would stay in the room all day, sitting beside my mother's bed and keeping her company. I even learned how to crochet and began to make my mother a blanket out of all those little squares.

Mom had worked for G. C. Murphy when she first came to Alexandria, so she would tell me, "Cernata, go get your lunch there…" because all the waitresses knew me. Towns were smaller then, so parents wouldn't mind their children walking a block or two to get groceries or run an errand to the pharmacy. Alexandria was a little, quaint town, and our family had been there a long time. But I would scarf my lunch down and get back to the hospital quickly because I didn't want her to be by herself. Of course, my grandmother, father, and sister visited daily, but she loved especially her son-in-law's visits with the little girls, my nieces, who would wave up to her from the parking lot. They weren't allowed to come in the hospital. It broke her heart not to be able to touch her grandchildren.

I can't help but remember my conversation with my mother just before she died, when she was preparing me for life ahead without her, giving me advice; about what doctor to call, this and that. She tried to introduce the subject of boys—with the notion that I was going to start liking them—until I interrupted: "I hate boys!" (Because they were always harassing me about my glasses and my chubbiness). And of course there was a reminder: "You know sometimes your father doesn't always do the right thing, but that's your father…" Fifty years later, I see that even as she lay dying, she was still cleaning up after everybody!

On her deathbed, in the early hours of the morning, she said her goodbye to my father and extracted a promise: "Take care of Cernata, my baby girl."

I never did finish making that blanket. All those crocheted squares…what became of them?

They were displaced, just like my life. In pieces. Each square meant time spent at my mother's bedside; I couldn't look at one without pain, deep-down and twisting.

~

When my mom died our entire family fell apart. Her need to fix her family's mistakes, especially my father's and sister's, affected us all. If my sister made a mistake—my mother was right there to fix it. And the difference between my sister and me? When I needed it, no one was around to clean up my mess. Up ahead, you'll see me without shelter, without resources. Not even from the church, the beloved church to which our family had dedicated their lives and where I had, grown up. In crisis, there was no one close by to help.

Or so it seemed to me.

~

My grandmother, slipping into dementia, was abruptly moved to New York by her family—they wanted her as far as possible from the responsibility of raising a teenager, and away from my father. He'd starting drinking, spiraling out of control because he thought all our misfortunes were his fault. He blamed himself for my mother's death, and he found reason for that in the circumstances of the accident.

On that Sunday, he and my mom were traveling up to Baltimore to a building dedication for one of my aunts. My dad had asked my mom especially to come with him. It was just the two of them in the car. I have a troubling memory that both my nieces and I wanted to go too, but for some reason my mother said, "No, stay home and go to church with your grandmother!"

The police officer who spoke to my father indicated that if anyone had been in the back of the car, they would have died. (Seat belt laws were rarely enforced in 1972.) My two nieces and I would not have survived the accident, saved, I believe, by God's will and purpose.

My father carried the burden of his guilt for a long time.

He couldn't cope, but he knew he needed to do something.

CHAPTER FIVE

A SHORT INTERLUDE IN BOSTON

In a matter of thirty days I'd buried my mother, lost my grandmother to dementia and found myself packed up for Boston, Massachusetts, to live with a more financially secure branch of my father's family. I never got to say goodbye to my grandmother; I simply watched from afar, crying, as she got in the car that drove her away from us. No one waved back. The adults around me judged that her dementia would have made a hug goodbye too devastating for her.

They made that decision without consulting me.

I was enrolled in a Catholic school near Boston by my father's family. My father said that it was just for the summer, but I was being fitted for shoes and a new uniform…and placed on a strict diet in hopes of a better fit. The new uniform was the clue; this was no summer stay. I was going to be living up here.

From my new home up north, I put pressure on my daddy with regular phone calls.

"I don't wanna be here."

"Cernata, that is the best place for you." And he was probably right. Though I would beg him, *beg him* to come get me.

"I can't be the father that you need right now."

"Daddy, I'll help you." I wanted to help him. Because I knew he was a good person, and that he needed help right then.

He ended the conversation. "I can't honey, I just can't. I promised your mother I would take care of her baby girl."

But I got so angry. So angry. *Why is this happening to me,* I thought. *God! I didn't ask to be born.* Then I started threatening my dad, saying, "If you don't come get me, I'm gonna walk out of this house and y'all will never see me again."

From my aunt's home, I called my uncle in Boston and said, "I wanna go back home. I have to go back home."

And he said, "Cernata, we can't do that right now. We have to help our brother."

To which I said, again, "If y'all don't let me go back home, y'all are never gonna see me again. I'm gonna get *outta* here."

My uncle finally heard me, he got it: *this girl is distraught.* Speaking with my father, he was very clear. "Y'all have taken her from what she's familiar with. Nobody has explained anything to her. And then we're gonna just bring her to New England and think she's just going to accept everything that's going on?"

And the funny thing about it all is that this branch of my family always seemed to me like the perfect family; they were my "perfect cousins." But you know there was so much chaos going in their lives. I thought: *they crazy up here too!*

I see them now, good people trying to help. They gave me shelter when I needed it. Of course they weren't crazy. They were a family living a normal life in a household with teenagers. And I see me, young, bereft, hopeless, wanting so badly to be home.

Pretty soon, my dad got tired of me calling. And one day I took things into my own hands and launched my runaway strategy. My aunt was off to go to the doctor. I said to her, "I'll just stay here and practice the piano." Well, I had already packed my stuff. And with my good sense of direction I knew which way the highway was and I planned to hitchhike all the way back to Alexandria.

But my aunt came home early! And there I am: caught in mid-flight, walking down the street with my bags. Funny, actually, as I remember it.

There was some talk that I needed therapy. And I probably did. But nobody was paying that close attention.

I came back home. And boy here was a scene I had never anticipated. No way was I prepared for the level of chaos I encountered. So I had to look out for Cernata. It was like sending a lamb out among the wolves, only I was the one doing the sending. I had to learn to survive, real quick, on the streets, because the rest of the family were caught up in their own thing. With my father plunged in mourning, my sister had her own woes: she and my brother-in-law were divorcing, and she was very vulnerable. Struggling to make an impact at her job at Xerox, she fell gravely ill, and suffered a stroke. Truth is, without my mother, we were all lost.

And still nobody was paying attention to Cernata.

~

The street became my conduit to survival, because my dad would be spending all his money elsewhere and, most times, we wouldn't have food to eat. Just a roof over our heads. And was that enough for a growing teenage girl? I was often faced with having to be the adult, using the little social security check I'd gotten as settlement for my mother's death to buy food, clothes and whatever else I might need.

I remember my girlfriend, saying, "When my aunt goes upstairs to sleep, I'm going to get another plate and act like I'm eating. When I cut the light off in the kitchen, I want you to come to the back door." And she would pass me the plate of food, and I would sit eating on her step before walking back to my house. I mean, that went on for years. I couldn't focus in school, so I left, just dropped out, thinking my girlfriend and I'd be hanging out in DC. Or get jobs.

And how are we gonna get jobs at our age? As teenagers? Jobless, lost, I was in and out of the house, dodging my dad. He'd leave for work and I'd come home, wash, grab such fresh clothes and be gone again.

My life was a drama. And it's next chapter? "The Street."

CHAPTER SIX

THE STREET

c. 1973-1974

I didn't do drugs, I was never raped, but I was up close and personal with the street life. Just hanging in the wrong places with the wrong people.

Let me roll a short tape for you: I see somebody running out of a building late at night. A bullet comes whizzing by my head. I feel so close to death I can touch it.

Then, here I am again, watching someone drugging up—until God sends someone else to say, "You young girls have no business being on this street. Let's get you out of here."

I know God planted a hedge of protection around me back then. And through it all, the good my family gave me—the foundation—was still there. Something was tugging at my young girl's heart.

I could be sitting in the most irretrievable situation and I would hear my mother's voice, "Cernata you don't belong here. Get out." I could feel danger ruffling its feathers. Until one day I just said, "I can't do this anymore. This is not my life."

I had been listed as a runaway when I dropped out of high school, missing most of my 9th and 10th grades. Ducking my dad, ducking the truant officers. But I was tired. So tired. Felt like, this *cannot* be my life. But I didn't want to go back to my dad because he hadn't yet beat the alcohol. Nor was my sister, in deep depression from her divorce, in any shape to help. If she couldn't choose well in her own life, she wouldn't make good choices for me.

~

So I turned myself into the court system.

My girlfriend had been saying, "Don't do this, they're gonna lock you up, they're gonna put you in the juvenile!" And I said, "I can't run anymore."

I walked in the main courthouse on King Street. And they locked me up for truancy. (Back then they were strict on truancy and runaways.) I didn't know what would happen next. Maybe somebody would adopt me. *I just didn't know*! But here's an inkling … if my mother and my father and my grandmother were so heavily involved in church… where was the church? That's the question to ponder here.

In the meantime, and maybe this is the answer: my mom's best friend, Mom Louise, who was very involved in the church, really did try to reach out to me, but I would call her and then hang up. Or I'd call my nieces and they would be upset and crying, saying "Cernata, is this you?" Phoning was not easy in detention in the 70s—calling my nieces back was hard so they had no choice but to worry.

I was arrested, put in a car and taken to the juvenile detention center. I remember sitting in the back of that car, in handcuffs. I remember too, them taking me out of the car, while in my mind I'm talking to my mom, thinking: *this isn't my life*. But I'd been out of school, working here and there and hanging out in the streets for a few years, and I knew I couldn't go in crying. I couldn't go in soft.

I went in. They processed me…one of the most humiliating things I've ever experienced. You know they strip you down. Right? They strip you down and then they water hose you. Not to hurt you, but to clean you off, like an animal. And I was so angry at my father and my sister. So mad. *So mad.* I was NEVER going to forgive them for what was happening to me. Weren't they supposed to protect me?

I was given a jump suit, clean underwear, a bra. I got the cell at the end of the unit. We had breakfast in the morning, daytime activity, school, lunch. We could play ball and talk with our counselors. My counselor was frustrated, "We're trying to reach your father and your sister, but nobody's returning the call."

They let me sit in there almost a week.

Luckily I was in a cell by myself, which kept me safe. The only time I interacted with the general population was lunchtime, when we were heavily guarded. When I was in the cell, I prayed under my breath: *this cannot be my life, this is not who I was destined to be,* asking, *what has happened? God help me!*

One night I was lying there and I could hear the keys turning in the door to our unit. There was a woman walking toward me, saying, "Please tell me this isn't who I think it is. Lord, this can't be Catherine's baby. I have known this child all her life." It was Mrs. Dantley, a friend of my mother's. And she told the guard, "Open up this cell!" I sat up on the bed. She grabbed me and hugged me, and all the while I'm begging her to get me out.

She says, "Where is your father?!"

I said I didn't know, that I'd called and no one would come.

She says, "You're gettin' outta here."

Well, the next day I was sitting out in the "general population" and they called my name. I could see my father, but I was sectioned off from him and he could only see me through glass walls. I was wearing a jumpsuit. I saw him break down crying.

And the irony in all this? My father worked a few blocks from the detention center.

I was processed out. And I was mad. I was *livid* at my father and sister. I wanted to just go off on them, physically. When I told my story to my truant officer, she asked me if I wanted to go into foster care, and out of all this anger, I said yes. I said, "I can't live like this, I have to turn my life around."

We go to Juvenile Court, The City of Alexandria, Virginia.

Picture this now: The presiding judge is a client of my mother's sewing business, Judge Pancost. She says, "This cannot be Catherine Stanton's daughter." My father drops his head. "Do you mean to tell me that Catherine Stanton...one of the kindest hearted people in this community...that her baby is in the system!?"

My case officer wanted temporary custody of me. But my dad begged them, "Give me another chance, I don't want to lose my daughter, just give me another chance."

By now, I'm fifteen, sixteen. I forget. I don't want to remember.

~

Here's another inkling of what's to come...

My father did not sue the young boy who was involved in the accident that resulted in my mother's death. The boy was a teenage drunk driver, although drunk driving laws were not on the books at that time. Even so, the insurance company was responsible. The insurance company was going to award me, as the youngest in the estate, all the money. I said: divide it between my father, my sister and me, because we were all heirs. So, my father told my sister, "You're the one that's been to college, I want to make you the guardian of your sister's money."

The court agreed that all of my money would be put in a trust fund until I reached the age of 18, with the accumulated interest—everything—put in the Bank of Virginia. I'll never forget it. My sister was told that the account would be monitored, and any withdrawals would need to be recorded with receipts. For dental bills and the like. My sister was bonded by the Courts to protect my interest.

It was a substantial amount of money, approximately $75,000 in 1972, which at 2019 value, could be worth around $450,000. Or, imagine the value to a young girl in 1977, with compounded interest accumulating over 5 years?

Estimating it was well over $100,000...why that could buy a college education!

All under the guardianship of my sister.

CHAPTER SEVEN

THE SWAN
AND THE UGLY DUCKLING

My sister had a support system. Not just my mother, but my grandmother and father. No matter what she did, they were not going to let her fall. She will tell you to this day: "Cernata had the more challenging life growing up as a teenager, but she turned out the better person." At first, when she would say that, I would say, "You're crazy," remembering the times when I wanted my mom's attention so bad. But she would insist, "Cernata you are by far the better person," adding, "You could have turned out like me." And what did that mean? We will see.

Growing up in our family, my sister was the swan and I was the ugly duckling. She was my father's pride and joy, the child who had replaced the son he had lost, the one who'd had all my parents' attention for the thirteen years before I showed up. She was a star in high school: sang alto in the chorus, led the band as the drum majorette and played basketball. While I was a tomboy and overweight, a chunky girl, living in the shadow of my lovely sister. Wearing my thick glasses, I was bullied and constantly teased at school. And I never got a chance to talk about the struggles of these awkward years to my mom because she died so suddenly.

When Mama left this earth and transcended, it was like all the shields my sister had depended on were stripped away. Now what? What would you guess? My sister fell apart. She couldn't cope. Of course she was smart, scholarship smart. She'd married her childhood sweetheart, Roger, the tall, soft-spoken young man who would go to college in Missouri on a football scholarship; their baby was born just before they set off to attend college. But since my sister was an awkward new mother, it was my mom who would take over the care of the baby so my sister and her husband could continue their education. Roger dearly loved my mother and appreciated all she did to help them advance in life. My sister and her husband were true loves, but as far back as 1598, Shakespeare said, "the course of true love never did run smooth." And as I would discover much later when a love of theatre got hold of me, sometimes life is easier lived on stage, though its wisdom transcends the footlights.

~

You've seen me as a teenager, now see me at the age of four: I'm an aunt. Instead of having the attention that a four-year-old might expect from her parents, I have to share. I'm four years old, an aunt who feels like a big sister. Then when I'm six, my sister leaves her college study to travel to Missouri where her husband is studying…and produces a second child. My mom and dad take in that baby as well. And now here I am, six years old and an aunt twice over. But I don't mind because now I have company in our home in The Berg: my sweet nieces.

Yet I couldn't have understood the effect this was having on me. After some time apart, my sister and brother-in-law were back home working on being a couple again. At this time, I started feeling a kind of rivalry with my dear nieces and bristled at the loss of attention.

For example, my elders would say, "Cernata, you can't sit in the front seat. You're the big girl, let your baby niece sit upfront." A child notices these things, and I certainly took them to heart. Looking back, I recognize them as the first clear signs of resentment at my situation. I was observing everything, while others were seeing nothing. I saw my sister and brother-in-law in their own house in Falls Church, and sure enough there was my grandmother moving in with them to take care of their kids. I saw my mother, working all day cleaning other people's houses, then coming home to clean our house until it was pristine. Then she would pack me up, go over to Falls Church and clean *their* house. And do laundry. And cook a Sunday meal—while my sister and her husband were in bed asleep.

They loved each other, and they had family support, but even with all that support their London Bridge was falling down. Things would get worse.

Still, my sister was quite capable of surprise. And her next move would open up a long-closed chapter in all our lives.

CHAPTER EIGHT

THE MAN WHO WALKED AWAY

1971

We unspool time now to pick up the threads of a lost story. Remember "The Man Who Walked Away?" He was my mother's father. Our grandfather. And one day my sister dug him up. "What?!" you say. Yes, she dug into the matter, did her research and found the man who had walked away, leaving a wife and the small child who was my mother.

He had moved to Parkersburg, West Virginia and married a lady named Matilda. They had one son. Eventually the son also married and had a son.

Some fifty years earlier, back when he left my grandmother and disappeared, he'd founded a new family. He'd returned to them only once, mysteriously appearing when my mother was deathly ill with pneumonia. He'd stayed until she was well, only to disappear once again, and for good.

After my sister found him, my mother was able to reconnect with her father in circumstances best described as turmoil. Once found, he'd wanted to speak to my grandmother but she wanted nothing to do with him. All of us were supposed to go visit him that summer after we found him, but my mother died before we could get there. Matilda, his "second wife," never knew about the first family from Charlottesville. She was devastated by the news.

So, my sister dug deeper. Stepping up with her bold and courageous self, she looked up the uncle we never knew we had and found him in Manhattan. She even drove there with her boyfriend and knocked on his door. The uncle we didn't know we had, opened it.

And of course, he'd only recently learned about my mother, the sister he never knew existed. Aware that his own mother was in a bit of a tizzy, he chose his course.

To my sister standing in front of him, he said, "I don't have a sister in Virginia. I don't know who you are, and I couldn't care less about you or anybody else. Don't you ever come and knock on my door again."

My sister described the scene to me later: the lovely Caucasian woman standing next to him, the beautiful little boy looking on, and the moment when our "uncle" slammed the door in her face.

After my sister's adventure in Manhattan, my mother, being the person she was, said simply, "Don't bother him. It's not his fault. This is all a shock to everybody." Meanwhile, for almost a year, the man who walked away was trying to make up for lost time. He wrote my mother cards, he sent flowers, he sent pictures…he wrote two or three times a month. But when my mother, his long-lost daughter, would call, his second wife decided not to tell him. For years, he thought my mom just didn't want to be bothered with him. In the twisting and turning of events, he never got to rekindle his relationship with her. Later, he developed glaucoma and lost his sight. The irony is hard to miss: he would never see any of us again.

Although we tried. I would call and Matilda would answer with the same message, "He gets really upset when he talks to you… he's anxious, but he really wants to see you." Hmmmm. A few years passed, and I was determined to pick up the phone again. The number was disconnected, so I called the police station. Since Parkersburg, West Virginia was a small town, they were able to share the news immediately, "Mr. Webb? He died a couple of years ago."

I never got to go see him. Though thanks to my sister, we found out what had become of him, and a hole in our lives was filled.

It came to pass in his first conversation with my mother that he had asked for her forgiveness. My mother, still the person she had always been, did so. Then she moved on, looking forward to our trip planned for the summer of 1972, when she would finally reunite with her long-lost father.

She died before we could make that trip.

Yet the man who walked away had been found. She was at peace.

CHAPTER NINE

HEROES AND VILLAINS

c. 1975

I had survived the street and my short stint in the juvenile center. I went back to school and made up two years in about a year-and-a-half. I would often stay with my mother's best friend, Mom Louise, or with my godmother in DC, or at another friend's home. I was like a bag lady, dodging my dad, but it was what I needed to do to stay away from the environment back home. My father was still challenged; my sister was in some bad relationships and not making good decisions. Divorced and living on her own, she was in her late twenties through her early thirties during this time. Her kids were living with their dad and they all lived with his family. Though she had joint custody and was supposed to get them every other weekend, she didn't always make the visit.

This is a good moment to remember what I said in my foreword, dear readers: There are no heroes and villains in this account, unless there is a bit of each in all of us. My goal is not to hurt or defame, especially those closest to me, but to understand what was holding me back. Who was this Cernata who would allow others to shape her life? When and how would she finally break out and be the person God had destined her to be?

I was supposed to be getting a little check, my social security as a dependent meant to compensate for my mother's death. And my sister would have to sign it. Sometimes she would sign it, sometimes she wouldn't even give it to me, because there were bills to be paid. Like rent for our home in The Berg. Sometimes we would get into physical altercations, and I would get hurt. I thought to myself, *my sister is out of control.* I would soon find out why.

I decided to get a part-time job. Although I was only 16, I looked 18. I started working at the Bank of Virginia...and I worked hard. Bought my first car and made enough to put clothes on my back. For this latter part of my teenage years, I just wanted to have a normal life, though I was still struggling to accept myself as I was. *Not* lean, petite and cute, as the prevailing standards required. But *not* someone you'd try to bully. Truth was, everybody liked me; I was fun to be with, but I wasn't the girl the guy next door would want to date. In the midst of this search for my true self, my judgment may have been clouded.

I started dating the wrong kind of guy.

CHAPTER TEN

THE WRONG KIND OF GUY

c. 1975-1977

Here's where the pattern kicks in.

I've decided to go back to school. As part of trying to support myself, I get a job cleaning at night. I fall in love with this guy who is the brother of the owner of the cleaning company, a young man from North Carolina whom I shouldn't have been dating. He's violent and insecure, a little ashamed of Cernata because Cernata is a big girl, taller than he is, bigger than he is. At five-feet-seven to my six-feet, the guy is petite.

The relationship will span my late teenage years, ending while I am going to Howard University and working two jobs. He is a blue-collar worker. He's going through divorce and has an alcohol problem that often sends him spinning out of control. I live with his violent outbursts, the jealousy, and the abuse— both physical and mental. Back then, I'm not able to see that being a nice person is not the same as being someone you'd want to be in a relationship with.

Although a little guy, his ring finger size is 15. Imagine the size of that fist.

~

Something to consider: How does somebody as strong as Cernata keep being drawn to people like this? As a young girl up in Boston she wanted to go home to Virginia to help her Dad, even when she couldn't help herself. Did she catch that spirit from her mother and grandmother, sweet enablers so willing to sacrifice for others?

I look at that girl now: she had such low self-esteem. Folks today would say; Dr. Morse was that *you?* Because I stand tall. Six feet, barefoot, and statuesque. *Cernata*…I looked up the name…it means, "she is a warrior, she fights for what she wants." Yet I'd always felt that I was the underdog. I see myself as that young girl, never able to look in the mirror to find what I was looking for, the unique abilities that God had surely given me. Why was that? Was it by design?

I also see the man from North Carolina: he is very controlling. So, when I step up to say, "I'm leaving," he hits me in the face. While I am being rushed to the hospital the pain makes one thing clear. He has broken my jaw.

But this is not our first brawl. Over the span of the relationship it has become a pattern, complete with bruises and black eyes. Friends and classmates ask, "Why are you walking around with sunshades and it's cloudy outside?" Meanwhile, I am covering up the abuse, wondering, worrying about what others will think, though *not* worrying about the mentally fracturing things happening to me. Instead, I make excuses for the person who did this to me.

Why?

Because I loved him. Foolish? Perhaps. But he was my first love and I thought things would get better. Of course they didn't.

In the hospital, nursing my fractured jaw, I remember my father being furious and issuing a warrant for the perpetrator's arrest. I remember having police protection at the hospital, and that my boyfriend's mother was driven up from North Carolina to visit me. That too, I remember quite clearly. She is kind, petite, a beautiful lady; the mother of sixteen children.

She leans over my hospital bed to talk. My responses are limited since my jaw is wired shut. She prays over me and says these words: "Cernata, you deserve better. This is not your life. My son is sick and he needs help. I don't know why this is happening to you, but you've got to let him go."

She's crying and I'm crying. (This I'm able to do with my mouth wired shut.)

The very next day I am scheduled for surgery. There are two doctors. Twins: Ferris and Ferris. Oral surgeons with a practice in Alexandria. They had taken x-rays when I was admitted to the hospital and noted that, because of the way the jaw was broken, it couldn't heal while it was wired. Back in those days, to examine an X-ray properly, you had to hold it up to the light. I remember them looking at the image of my face, and talking to my dad. One says, "There is no other way to get in there except by cutting from the back of her right earlobe, along her jaw to her chin." They say they'll try to make the incision as neat as possible but plastic surgery will be the only way to remove the scar.

My dad is a blue-collar worker. He won't be able to afford plastic surgery. On a chair beside my hospital bed, he weeps.

The day of the surgery the twins come in again. They had asked for additional X-rays to check for any changes before beginning the procedure. Holding them up to the light, one asks the other, "Do you see what I see?"

And the other says, "Yes, but it makes no sense to me."

They look at it from a different angle. They adjust the light and turn the image around. Disbelieving what they're seeing, one says: "It's fusing back together."

They walk back over to my bed.

"Young lady, we're not going to operate," says one.

The other nods. "Your jawbone is fusing back together."

And I begin to cry, still not able to understand this intervention as a blessing from God. It's clearly a miracle, but even in the face of a miracle, in the very face of God's infinite power, I still have doubts about who I am.

They decide to leave my mouth wired shut for another eight weeks.

It heals completely. The trauma to my face leaves no trace. But my mind – the damage is irrevocable.

CHAPTER ELEVEN

GOOD PEOPLE,
BAD RELATIONSHIPS

What happened to the man who fractured my jaw? He left and went back to North Carolina. And the strange thing was, he became a minister. I will say, he had a hard life toward the end with death by kidney failure. But he called me, just before he got married for the second time. I was reluctant, but he begged to talk to me. I said, "What could you possibly want to talk about?" He said that God had told him to right his wrongs by asking for forgiveness.

And why am I even telling this part of the story? Because this was my first love, someone I loved profusely. (I can hear your *"Why!"*) Don't know why I did, but I did. I believe that the action he took, calling me to ask for forgiveness, and my being obedient to God by accepting it, was necessary. I needed to say the words out loud: "I forgive you." This lesson was planted in my life journey for a purpose…because it wouldn't be too long before I would be asking for forgiveness just as he did.

At the time he called, I was married and in love with my husband. I had one child and another on the way, and, in that moment, I almost laughed it off, wondering why, after all these years, this man is calling and asking for forgiveness. I didn't know what it meant; I didn't know how monumental it would be, but I remember it as if it had happened yesterday. I guess I had enough of The Holy Spirit in me to hear what he said. His last words were, "You know I made you feel so bad as a young girl. But you are, inside and out, one of the most beautiful people I have ever met. Cernata, you are special. And I pray that you are happy with your husband and family. I will forever love you!"

That was the last time I spoke with him.

~

Fast forward: I'm really close now to his oldest daughter. She loves me "to life." And I love her just as much. She reminds me so much of him, of the *good* man I fell in love with. And you know, she will just shake her head and say, "I don't know why my dad didn't see the value in the relationship with you."

And I say, "You know what? Good people. Bad relationships."

CHAPTER TWELVE

BONE DRY

1977

I am 18 years old. I've survived the street life; an abusive relationship and I've made up for lost time in high school. I even have a job. Now I'm at the threshold of my dream: I will escape Alexandria at last and go to California to study. Although I've applied to Howard University and some others, I've been accepted at UCLA and another college in Virginia.

I tell my Dad, "I'm getting outta here. I'm gone." And he says, "Why do you want to go so far?" Perhaps he is haunted by my plan to leave because he doesn't trust himself. Though he's really slowed down with the alcohol, he is still unpredictable. He's a good man, my father, but with the alcohol he's like Dr. Jekyll and Mr. Hyde.

It is time to go.

I tell my sister, "I need to go to the bank and get my money." But she keeps putting it off, giving no reason, just putting it off. Meanwhile I'm calculating the value of the fund. Six years' worth of interest. I should have enough to help me go to school for four years. I've even bought a little ticket to put my car on a train. I have worked so hard at my part-time job at the bank, and making up my high school classes after those lost years in the street. All of it, all of it to be able to do this: I'm going to California! Got my roommate. Everything is set to go. I am going to do it. I'm scared but I am going to do it.

And then one day she calls.

My sister is irate; I can tell she has been drinking.

"There is no money."

And I say, *"What?"*

She's like, "You don't have any money. It's all gone."

"What!" I say. You talkin' about mad? I am mad. I say, "Nuh, nuh, nuh, nuh, no! This **&^^%% ain't happening. This cannot be happening."

But of course it was, and it had.

She had used up every dime. The guy who she was dating at the time was into the criminal scene and knew all the crooked judges. He knew all the bent people down at the courthouse who kindly turned a deaf ear so that my sister was able, over the course of six years, to drain my life savings dry.

Bone dry.

What happened to be being bonded and a juvenile protected by the courts?

Did she need the money? Well, she was working, but she was also partying. Just living the life.

I go to my dad. "Daddy this cannot be happening."

"What did you say?" And so, he calls her. She comes back at him, still irate and irrational. "I don't care if you put me in jail…" She's in a state of denial, trying to explain what happened, as if any of it could make sense.

I go to my godmother and say, "Why is God punishing me? *What did I do?*"

I just could not believe it. My father and my godmother come to talk to me, because I am distraught.

My godmother is talking through her tears: "Cernata, I'm telling you, God brought you into this world for a reason. And it's beyond our comprehension. He has a calling on your life…" Now *I'm* crying. While she keeps going, "The Enemy has been trying to destroy you from a young age! But Baby, I am trying to tell you that God is going to bless you beyond measure. And you're going to be able to tell the world what a mighty God we serve."

She says, "I don't know why this is happening to you." She says, "It makes no sense to me or your father. I know your mother is turning over in her grave. Your sister has gotten everything handed to her...how could she do this to her sister? How could she do this to her *baby* sister!...who has suffered since the time her mother has closed her eyes."

But she also says this: "Cernata, you can't do evil for evil." Because I was livid. I was ready to take my sister to court. Like, how much more can you take, right?

Like, all I do is give. All our lives, my nieces and I, we've been close. When they have soccer games and basketball games, I am the one who is always there. At 17 and 18, I am the one who is giving them money for their little school trips, because my sister fails them from time to time. I am the one who comes to pick them up when my sister leaves them stranded in the middle of the night, because they're off at a concert, and she doesn't feel like leaving where she is.

While I, with my young, broken-hearted voice say, "She's crazy! *My sister, she just crazy.*"

I remember asking God, "How could she be doing this to me?"

CHAPTER THIRTEEN

EVIL FOR EVIL

Fast Forward to 2019

Now in my wisdom years I speak with a different voice; I ask different questions. I wouldn't use the words, "she just crazy" to describe my sister. But I do wonder, what drove her to do what she did? When did her good judgment abandon her? Because we were not raised that way.

It's been a long time coming, but the relationship has improved. Still my memory sees it occasionally as it once was. Raveled, like a piece of rope, hard used. I've come a long way since I asked God to allow me to forgive her and put that past behind me.

There are times in our conversations when she reminds herself of the mistakes she made in life; she feels guilty. She says it was the alcohol, her bad judgment in men, and that she was just *out there*. Lost. Equally often, that young girl in me wants to step up in protest: "What were you thinking, honey? How could you just blow that much money?!" But the wise woman in me chooses more measured questions, "Why did you *need* that much money? What was going on in your life that led to those bad decisions?

She doesn't have a good answer for that one.

But I'm pretty sure the guys she was around were taking advantage of her. (One in particular, we'll call The Influencer.) My sister has the same foundation I have, laid down by our parents and grandmother. She witnessed the love, the sharing and caring and, most importantly, the sacrifice. But something must have happened. Maybe her life too, was bent out of shape by others' expectations. She was the only child for over thirteen years. Our parents and grandmother did everything for her. Was this her expectation of what life would always be like?

At the time it was all happening, she'd say, "I'm working hard and I'll put all the money back." But how can you put all that back?

~

Meanwhile, in 1977, at age 18, I'm facing the ruination of my plans. The dream is gone. I couldn't even spell the word.

Dream.

I couldn't see it in front of me anymore. Gone. Pouf.

I'm distraught; my father is unbelieving. He is so proud of me for turning my life around. But I'm in such a state, that even though my father and godmother have come over and cried with me, I don't want to hear it. They're telling me I can't do evil for evil. And, I'm thinking, *I'm gonna throw her and her boyfriend in jail.* This is ridiculous. I'm a kid! Hadn't I experienced enough hard times? Don't I deserve a chance to be successful?

~

So, I go to this lawyer on Vermont Avenue in D.C. I'm mad.

The lawyer, he sits and crosses his legs. "Ms. Stanton, this is a very unfortunate situation. It really disturbs me how the court system has failed you." (Remember now, my sister was bonded. She was supposed to be looking after my interest.)

"If what you're telling me is the truth, you're going to be the richest little black girl in the state of Virginia." He looks me dead in my face and says, "Because not only can you sue the bonding company, you can sue the lawyers, and the state—which, by the way, has failed you horribly. But here's the catch. Your sister's going to go to jail for a *long* time...and that's what you've got to be ready for. Whether she had somebody do this for her or what, we're talking about a federal...a criminal...case."

He keeps going, "You're going to come out ok in the end, and what else? People are going to come to you, because they're going to try to buy your story."

He said that. I'll never forget it.

He said, "Because this is the stuff that TV is made of."

~

I leave that office in total shock. I'm upset, scared and worried all at once. Why am I being placed in this situation? Once again, I get angry at God.

I go back and tell my father what the lawyer said. And he cries. I am looking at my father getting down on his knees and crying out to God. "I've failed my family. How did my oldest daughter do this to her baby sister! What have I done to my daughters?"

My father begs me.

My godmother begs me. "Cernata, think about her children, her daughters. Y'all are so close. But this is going to destroy them, and the entire family."

Fine. Point taken. But what about me? No one seems to care about me. Why is all this happening? Hadn't I gone through enough in my teenage years? Going to California was supposed to be my big break, my chance to move away from Alexandria, Virginia. I wanted to glance at my rear-view window and see those bad memories sliding out of sight. I thought I'd come to the crossroads with a turn for the better just ahead.

Yet destiny wrote the next act: I would stay at home with the scars, the new trials life had in store, and just keep on walking. Long legs can cover a lot of ground. (It's amazing what you find when you keep on walking.) And everywhere is walking distance with God.

~

I pondered my choices for a long time. Was I going to go to court and plunge my sister into the criminal justice system? Resentful Cernata wanted to take things into her own hands and get revenge. But there was something else inside of her, something that could not be ignored. A light. A mother's sweet spirit and love of Christ and family. And a grandmother's constant reminder: "Everyone is a sinner saved by grace."

I pivoted. I found something new to believe. I just needed to tap down into our roots, down to the bedrock of our family. There, in the memory of my mother's eyes, I found what I needed. She was always thinking about everybody else's good. And she had planted that in me, that foundation of Jesus' love of mankind.

I didn't pull the trigger. I wouldn't go to court. I just couldn't ruin all our lives.

~

But I remained very angry for many, many years. I resented my sister for a trunkful of reasons. I came to a point where I would avoid her presence. I hated what she had done to me, snatching away my future. Over time the anger built up and up. I *really* resented her. The older I got, the easier it became to slash back with my razor-sharp tongue.

"I'm not going to tolerate any more bullying. I'm taking charge of my life."

But intention, by itself, is rarely enough when taking action is stymied. I knew I was smart in my own right; I would have done wonderful things out West.

Eager as I was to leave the East Coast and the burden of memory, I stayed where I was, still struggling; trying to go to school at Howard

University. Lucky even to keep my job at the bank. It seemed more was asked of me, a long hard road to travel, with thunderclouds massing up ahead.

CHAPTER FOURTEEN

THE MATCHMAKER

c. 1972

It is time to meet my father again. And to do that we return to 1972, to one of the pivotal moments of my life. It was the year my mother died and, with her gone, I get a new, up close and personal view of my father's journey in life. Before that year, I had known him simply as this tall, extremely handsome man who happened to be a blue-collar worker. I also knew his story. He was the baby boy of fifteen siblings of which only five were boys. You'll recall that the women in his family were dominant in all aspects of their lives.

My father had a meek and mild side to him and yet, when he consumed alcohol, another person would rise from the ashes of that meek side. This person was wild, carefree and perfectly capable of making reckless decisions.

Since my birth, up to the point of my mother's death, our family was very close-knit. Our entire household was focused on family and God, which translated to a social life mainly in the church and our schools. Our family was not perfect, but there was love there. I remember tough times and arguments between my parents but, somehow, they always worked through it. Still, in that dreadful year of 1972, everything fell apart.

With my mother's death and my grandmother's departure to her family in New York, the dynamics in the household had changed. Home was not really "home."

Trying to make sense of my situation, I'll admit to making some bad decisions myself. Clearly, I did not have a good sense of judgment about relationships, of the elements needed to make a successful match. It would take decades to figure that out, to develop the right gauge for a good relationship. "Why" is the million-dollar question. Was it because I was in a family of "goodwill enablers" who never dealt with the issues of dysfunction? Or had I learned how to filter, seeing only "the good" qualities of a person while hoping the bad behavior would go away.

~

Through the late 70s and early 80s, in my late teens to early twenties, working, going to school, I had been partying a lot, and my dad was concerned. He noticed I wasn't home much. Well, I didn't want to be home because "home" wasn't home to me. I mean I partied *a lot.* I had many friends who were male, but not one special boyfriend. I just partied. I've always been a dancer; I just love to party. You get the picture. But I was moving in the wrong circles. Once again, I was in a zone of danger. The fast life. The limelight. The city life in D. C. Wasn't doing the drugs but I *was* a party girl. All the clubs. Even when I brushed close to death, in the wrong place at the wrong time, God sent an escape. I was outta there. Or somebody *got me* outta there. Sometimes, when reports came back that bad things had happened, I'd remember being at that club. I'd feel the danger, its feathers ruffling my skin, when I realized I'd left it just ten minutes earlier.

~

My party life was wearing on me and I was ready for change. Not that I hadn't been busy: I'd caught up with my high school class at T. C. Williams and graduated on my original schedule. Enrolled at Howard. Gotten out of a bad relationship.

But now what? What was the next sharp turn my path was bound to take?

Living with my father after he began to minimize the drinking, actually became a little challenging. Especially after my ordeal with my first love. Dad had started to indicate that he wanted me to settle down and meet a "nice" man. And, sure enough, there was this one guy he'd noticed who seemed to be a good, hard-working guy, always pleasant to his customers. He would chat with my dad all the time.

Dad arranged a casual meeting with this young man as a way for us to be introduced. He had seen me one day when I picked up my father from work. He inquired about me and that was all my dad needed to hear.

CHAPTER FIFTEEN

I MEET THE MAN I WILL MARRY

c. 1981

When I first met him, he had a smile on his face, with the prettiest eyes I'd ever seen. Tall, handsome, soft-spoken, caring and loving, he was just a good ol' country boy from Southwestern Virginia. And he wanted all the same things I did. He wanted to marry, raise a family. He was always telling me how beautiful I was. He said that he liked big girls, that I was beautiful just the way I was. It was so...refreshing.

I remember our first date. He had on brown hush-puppies, green socks, brown corduroy pants, and he picked me up in a black and white ragtop Lincoln Mark IV. And we went bowling. I just noticed that he was very polite: did I want something to eat, something to drink? He brought me right back to the door at the end of the evening. The perfect gentleman, very kind-hearted. Months into dating I was sure that I was seeing him right. So, when he asked the question, I grabbed for my answer.

"Yes, I'll marry you."

~

Why did I say yes so quickly?

Because he was such a gentleman. And so nice-looking. Tall, and neat as he could be. But I did not look beyond the surface. I did not take the time to know him. It moved too quick. As the Bible says, you must look beyond the present to see beneath. Not to forget that, if he had looked closer at my family, he might have made a different decision as well. It goes both ways. You could say that the way the relationship started was wrong.

Now that I'm older and wiser I see more. But back then, when he introduced me into his family, they being country people and me a city girl, I was embraced by some and rejected by others. For whatever reason, my father-in-law adored me. Though I noticed the dominance of this man, he was also someone to be admired: a social activist, truly a powerful man. You could tell he was bound for greatness. But he was dominant; there was no doubt about who was the boss in that family.

My husband-to-be had grown up within that family dynamic. If it became his model, guiding his own family life, why would we be surprised?

CHAPTER SIXTEEN

UNPLANNED, NONETHELESS, A MIRACLE

c. 1982, Old Town, Alexandria, Virginia

This fine young man from Southwestern Virginia and I want to get married, and we want to do it on his birthday, which is July 24th. His sister is also planning her wedding, and wants to do it the same day, July 24th, 1982. I'm like, "*No!* I'm not going to be in a double wedding. And I'm not going to have it in the southwestern part of Virginia. My friends and family are up here."

So, we decide on a date. We will wait and marry a week before Christmas.

Well…

I get pregnant and I don't know it; don't even suspect it, because I'm taking the pill, and I think I'm safe, right?

But here's what happens; it does make for an instructive story, dear readers.

We are in the church one Sunday for counseling, and to schedule the dates for our wedding. My intended and I are sitting in the balcony at my old home church. And there's a part of the service where you stand up. I am wearing a white suit.

Suddenly my fiancé, who was always well-dressed, takes off his jacket and starts to put it around me.

I say, "What?"

And he says, "Oh my God. You're bleeding…there's blood all over your dress." We rush out of the church and he drives me to the hospital.

Our regular doctor, Dr. Edgar Lacayo is not on duty.

Now this is where people can wonder, this or that. Was it magical thinking? But this is a true story. With my fiancé as my witness. At the hospital, the doctor on call checks me in and then starts theorizing.

"I just think you need a DNC, because of the pill and everything, I think your body is just"…some medical term he uses. "You just need to get a DNC. We can schedule it later in the afternoon, whenever we can get you in."

Suddenly, it's gone quiet. Seems like everyone has disappeared, because there is *nobody* around.

And then this other doctor walks in, an older one. He says, "Hi, Ms. Stanton, how are you?"

I say, "Fine. I just don't know what's going on" and he says, "I'm looking at your reports." (By this time, they'd done blood work and other tests, including a sonogram.) And he says, "I don't think you should have the DNC today. If I were you, I would wait until tomorrow."

He says, "I'm getting ready to head off. But I know your regular physician, Dr. Lacayo, and he will be here tomorrow. I think he would want to make that determination. I understand you're thinking about going on and letting them do a DNC. I wouldn't do that today."

And my fiancé says, "Well we can wait."

Then more nurses come by; they're ready to schedule the DNC, when I tell them about this doctor who recommended otherwise. My fiancé and I describe him. To which they reply, "We don't know who that is. We've never seen him before." And I say that he was just here talking to us

Silence. It's like everyone is on PAUSE. Or, maybe everyone is trying to figure out who is crazy. My fiancé and I throw a quick look at each other.

It gets busy again; there are people flying all over the place. The nurses proceed to tell us that we have the right to deny the procedure. "You don't have to have this DNC now. Dr. Lacayo comes on in the morning, he'll be on call. You can speak with him then."

Next morning, sure enough, Dr. Lacayo is there. Tall. Impressive. Excellent bedside manner! (He'd turn out to be one of my best doctors, helping me birth my first two children. A good Christian from somewhere in Central America. I remember him as a gentle giant.)

To which he says, "There's nothing going on."

And I, voice rising, say "*What?!* They told me it's a blood clot!"

And he replies—so calmly—and with a smile, "No, that's not a blood clot. That's a baby."

My fiancé and I look at each other again.

I'm scared. He is overjoyed.

Now one of the things that drew me to him—and here's where it breaks my heart—is that he wanted all the same things I wanted. He loved the simple, good, things in life. And he loved me right where I was. He admired my size. I don't know how else to say it. He made me feel that I was loved. And he wanted a family.

So here I am standing with my mouth open: "Oh, my God what am I gonna do? I'm pregnant!! What will the church say?" I panic. "Everybody will…"

I'm gonna pause the story here for a minute to remind you one more time that I was always thinking about what everybody else would be thinking. *Always* worried about that. And so ashamed. Happy, but ashamed. And afraid that somebody was going to make me do something I didn't want to do.

But my fiancé was right there to say, "You're going to have the baby, and we're still going to get married."

"I can't get married in the church, this is embarrassing, people are going to be talking…"

Back at church, we tell the pastor. And he says, "Well, the baby's going to be born on such and such a date and y'all are going to get married, and y'all will need to come in for counseling; it's already on the books." Whatever else he said, I just heard, *blah, blah, blah.* Confusion and doubt plague me, but in the midst of it the thought arises that something needs to be made right, and I am the one to do it. I'd seen it all before as a little girl, situations like this where somebody was trying to make it right. Every time something went a little off track.

Unplanned, if you will. But before *this* unplanned, none the less a miracle, happened, I actually did feel my life was, finally, running on track.

CHAPTER SEVENTEEN

VINEGAR AND WATER

Winter 1982, Alexandria, Va

It is a beautiful winter day. Crisp air, sunshine. Imagine, a week before Christmas and there's no snow.

For months, we've been planning our wedding; my soon-to-be husband has been involved in every detail. We have worked together to make sure it will be the wedding of our dreams. All of his brothers are in the wedding, along with one sister, one sister-in-law, one cousin and his best friends. On my side I am represented by my nieces, best friends and a co-worker.

I do remember that the closer we got to the wedding date, the more I felt uncertain about what was about to happen. I worried that I might not be a good wife. My husband-to-be assured me I'd be o.k.

There were some reasons for my doubts, some early indicators of past baggage still being carried around by both of us. Like unresolved things in his previous relationship, eye-opening confrontations with his ex, and the tendency he'd developed to point out my flaws. My willingness to overlook all this had its reason. I wanted so much to relish this moment of true love.

After all, I was abused in that first relationship with the man from North Carolina. I never got counseling, because I didn't want anyone else besides close family to know what had happened to me. I stuff my doubts into some hard to reach part of my brain.

So here I am, on my wedding day. The car is waiting, the family is gathered at my father's house in Alexandria. And I'm in the middle of a breakdown. Not ready to jump back into a committed relationship. To tell the truth my soon-to-be husband isn't either, but it's too late, we're forging ahead. I feel as if some joke of a puppet-master is pulling my strings, that I'm not in my own body. No genuine self anywhere to be found.

My dad, my aunts, my nieces, his family, my best friends and bridesmaids are all ready to get into the cars. My sister is already at the church.

We arrive at the front door of the church. My dad is beside me, ready to walk me down the aisle. For the past few hours, he's been whispering in my ear. "He's a good man."

And he *is* a good man.

Of course we go through with the ceremony. But early in the marriage it becomes clear that my husband and I are vinegar and water. I have that strong independent streak, at a time when I have to depend on him financially. After all, I haven't yet finished school.

~

Let's call it "early warning system failure." In the beginning, what had attracted me to this charming southern guy was his gentleness and desire to be a family man. Only later did I learn there was history. (He had been married, and not yet secured a divorce when we met and started dating.) As with all of us perhaps, when we want something bad enough, we can overlook what we want not to see. In my case, for once, it seemed, I'd found someone who was attracted to me just the way I was. I certainly had flaws, and he didn't neglect to point them out to me. (That should have been a hint.) But I overlooked this, because I was still locked into a pattern of ignoring my better instincts about behavior that should have triggered alarm.

I'd met his family and thought, *whenever a guy takes you to meet his family, it's truly a committed relationship, right?* His family were very close-knit, the dad being its leader, as I've mentioned, the dominant personality making all the decisions. The mother had a very sweet, humble spirit and was always focused on "Dad" and the family as a whole. There were eight siblings, with my husband number three from the top. About a year after meeting his family we got married, and my life—to understate the truth—has never been the same. It would become a nearly three-decade-long mosaic of darks and brights, of good times, bad times, life-changing times, and pivotal, eye-opening moments.

Not long after the wedding, the early warning system did report on events happening between me and my new husband. Worrying events. But I was young, soon to be a new mother, and consumed by doubts about my ability to take on that role. When I could spare a moment to face those doubts, I could only conclude that part of my identity was still missing. I wanted more in life for myself and for my children. I just knew there had to be more to do, to be, to achieve.

CHAPTER EIGHTEEN

PURE BLESSING

1983

Ready or not, the day came: May 12, 1983. Our son was born. He came as pure blessing. And I knew that his being here was perfect, even as my whole life changed. I was like, "Oh, my God. I am a mother." An instinct kicked in, telling me that I had better be the very best mother I could, to nurture this little person into being his best.

I wanted my own mother to talk to, but I only had me. I would sit and lecture myself. "Look, you have got to survive for the sake of your child, this beautiful baby boy." But I noticed all the things that were changing. My husband exerted more control once I had the baby, over what I could do, couldn't do, what I could wear, couldn't wear. I may have been in a fog of new motherhood, but I knew well enough I wasn't that girl, the one who would take orders. There was always something in me; I was different. Don't know if it developed out of my time on the street—all the things I'd been and done before I met my husband—or something else, deep within. But what? Maybe this: I always wanted to be my individual self. I wanted to prove to all the naysayers in my life that I *could* be successful despite the odds I had been dealt. In my married years I didn't know what that might mean, but I would always buck up against anyone and any attempt to control me.

~

My husband turned out to be a dominant father. This was HIS son. He was going to give his son *this, this and this*, the classic stuff. He was from the old school. And I was, as we've seen, a little different. My hopes were simple enough. I just wanted our son to be highly educated, and to have all the opportunities I didn't get. Thus, one of my prayers right from the beginning was, *"God, whatever you do…and I know my time must come…please don't take me away from my child until he is an adult."* That became my prayer for each one of my kids. I never wanted them to go through what I had, losing a parent at a young age. And that prayer turned into the conviction that became the underpinning of my marriage. That's what kept me in it. I must admit, too, that I wanted my children to have a "solid" family life, unbreakable, unmovable, and always with both parents in the same house.

But who was I fooling? To make that work, both parents must be happy and, in my opinion, rooted in God to weather the storms of life. As we would too soon find out, our roots weren't deeply planted enough for the marriage to withstand coming storms.

~

Our new son was the first child to be born in our extended family in a long time. It had been a span of about twenty years since my nieces were young. Now they were up and grown and in college, one at a local computer tech college and the other at the University of Maryland, where she became a basketball superstar. These two nieces of mine were like my sisters. They did everything with me, and for me, including helping with the baby. They were wonderful to us. (I've always loved my nieces and to this day they have a special purpose in my life, as we'll see.)

But I was missing my mom so bad. No surprise that I slid into depression. So much so that Dr. Lacayo said that he wanted me to go to a therapist. I protested, of course, "Everybody's going to think I'm crazy." He reassured me that I was not. "Your body is going through a lot. You're missing your mom…" He was right on it. Mom Louise had tried to step in and help, but there is nothing like having your own mom at your side when you're a first-time mother, right? Even my mother-in-law would call and try to coach me through the uncharted waters of motherhood. Sadly, it didn't measure up to having my mother by my side when the other person on my other side was a baby. So, I buckled in with all my emotions strapped close to my chest, and chose to cry when no one was looking.

Or just pray my way through the pain.

CHAPTER NINETEEN

SCENES FROM A MARRIAGE

Fairfax County, Va

In 1984 we moved into our first home. In 1989 we moved again, into the home that would be ours for the next twenty-five years. My husband was a hard-working man. He loved his kids, unconditionally. This might not be a good analogy now, but, then, we were the Huxtables of our community—a hard-working, middle class African-American family. I was extremely active in the community with the kids. Picture this: in a year when I'm quadruple-tasking: I'm the treasurer of the PTA at the elementary school, the parent-liaison for the middle school PTA, and the graduate liaison and PTA Vice-President for the high school. There was nothing that my husband or I would not do for the betterment of our kids. Since we both had seen the opportunity for education taken from us at a young age, we determined that we would never let that happen to our kids.

He was working from the old adage: "Go to school, do your chores, when you're eighteen you're on your own, go to college, no excuses." I saw it a little differently. I wanted them to have a well-rounded life. So, I was the one pushing Little League baseball, soccer, track, community this, community that, in short, a well-rounded experience. He and I both wanted our children to be part of a community in ways that were reflective of America. All of it.

My husband sometimes worked at night, and would then come home in the day and work some more in a garage as a mechanic. I too could be found working occasionally at night. For twelve years, from 1989 to 2001, I had a responsible job in at PBS, at first as an executive assistant and then in production management. When the creatives needed to get something done and, on the air, it meant late hours. It was my father who stepped in to help; always there to help two working parents get done what needed to get done. He made that possible, reassuring everyone that he'd have dinner ready. And bless him, his dinners were like…Little Caesar's pizza! And Slurpees from 7-11! Of course the kids loved having him around; he was the best possible granddad. He was there every day. Took the youngest to school. Got them all off the school bus in the afternoon. My father was phenomenal. And my husband adored him. (They really loved each other.) We had a beautiful home down in the Bucknell area of Fairfax County and I mean we were a good, wholesome family.

Or so, it appeared.

~

Together we allowed Satan to step in. Both my husband and I are to be held accountable for the demise of our marriage. I will never blame my husband for everything and he can never blame me. Then, I was the kind of person (and thank God I've grown past that) who, if you do something to me, I will do it right back at you. It was just a vicious cycle. Truly vicious. Over time our relationship became so tattered and torn that every time, when it seemed it might be on the mend, something would happen and it would tear apart again, heading to the point of no return. I knew eventually we were going to get divorced; I just didn't know when. I didn't know how. I did know that I would fight for my kids. Seeing the storm ahead, I'd resolved that no one was going to take my children from me.

~

We'd married when I was in my early twenties. He was the elder by six years. It was his second marriage. And our family started the next year with the arrival of our son.

Two years later I would become the mother of a beautiful baby girl. She was my anchor child, adored by both her parents. Always a daddy's girl, she was the loving one who would become the perfect middle child, the peacemaker. She was the creative, left-handed child who loves to cuddle with her dad and me.

Four years later I would become a mother again to another beautiful baby girl. This one turned out to be adventurous and feisty. Always exploring and watching her big brother (six years older) and sister (four years older). The baby of the family, she claimed that title with relish, letting everyone know how things were going to be. Sure enough, both her older siblings became protective of her in all aspects of her life. She developed a strong voice of reasoning because she was a born observer, watching closely everyone else's actions, including mommy's and daddy's. Though she too was a daddy's girl, she was always up under mommy! She was hanging close to me all the time.

My "Morse Crew" was complete and now I had to fight for their well-being as well as their mom's!

~

From about ten years on, the marriage felt like it was ending. A long slow, sad, fade to black. When we'd been married almost fifteen years, we were at the breaking point. I was nearly forty.

Was there a single time or incident that made me feel uneasy in this union? Honestly, I started doubting myself the moment we got married, as I've recounted. Remember the breakdown on my wedding day? (The car waiting, the family gathered?) It wasn't that I didn't love him. I *loved* him. But something didn't feel right. Was it that old low self-esteem devil at work in me? In they rolled, the doubts, the fears. I wondered: *is this going to be just like everything else in my life? Are the surprises going to come and I can't handle them?* Doubting myself.

I think what happened was simple, in retrospect. Throughout the marriage I was trying to be something I wasn't. Inevitably, the real Cernata started bucking back. I resented being bound in a situation. Not of my choosing? But I chose it! Perhaps I still had some of the party girl thing going on. I do know that when I became a new mother, I wasn't ready. Everybody kept telling me: your husband, he's a good man. But there was an ancient double-standard in play, the old adage that women don't challenge men. If he's a good man, provides shelter and puts food on the table, that's all you want. And I was like, where did *this* come from?

You have to remember that I came up, not only in the Black Power movement, but in the time of women's empowerment. Women wanted to snatch off their bras, to have equal rights, equal pay. I was right on the cusp of baby boomers and Gen X. (If I'd been born a year later, I would have been a Gen Xer.) I think more like a Gen Xer. And now, in my wisdom age, I love being around the millennials in my personal and professional life. (Saying this makes me want to laugh, because sometimes millennials drive me crazy, but I do learn a lot from them. I love it.) They're always in "fast, quick and let's get it done" mode. "What's the easiest, quickest way to achieve success?" That's what they're looking for. Innovative and creative; they want to find a good outcome quickly. Gen X-ers understand there is a process: "Tell me what it is and I'll do it". Baby boomers are more analytical; they take their time thinking a process through. The veterans have the wisdom and knowledge, but they believe that learning and gaining experience over time is the way to be efficient, productive, and successful: "You must earn your stripes. That's what I did." Over the years, having spent time in academia, that side of me has helped me learn to embrace the differences in these four generational behaviors.

But of course, all this is way in the future. Let's rewind.

~

Together we were building our dream. My husband was very entrepreneurial, a good business man. But when he would come up with a new idea, he would always want to throw me in the middle of it, saying, "Cernata, you could manage this part of the business." And I would resent that. I would go, "This is not *my* dream. I don't want to do that." After all, I had lost my dream when I was ready to go to college the first time and the possibility up and vanished. Then, when I became a wife and mother, I had to let that dream go, again.

Look at all that was going on back then: I was a wife, brand-new mom, part-time college student and enmeshed in the constant struggle to be myself.

Okay, when do I have time to breathe?

~

My husband. You talk about a "southern rules" guy? That was him. I'm talking to my sister on the phone and she's laughing because she's just asked me what I am doing.

It's late at night, and I'm sounding frustrated.

"Well, I just put the baby down, and I'm cooking."

"What're you cooking?"

"Fried chicken, green beans, mashed potatoes, and I'm making some biscuits."

"At 8:00 at night?"

"Yeah, but, he doesn't like instant mashed potatoes, and I had to soak the chicken…"

And she's like, *"Uh, what?!"*

~

Well that stuff got old real quick. So, by the time my third child was born, I said, "This is how we're gonna do this. I'm gonna make a big pot of spaghetti…" Even so, I needed to be creative because, once our family was complete, I had four + me at the table, all of whom had different tastes in cuisine.

To be fair there would be times when my husband would take the family out to dinner, just to give me a break. And I soon learned from people like Mom Louise to make a meal to last two days. But on Sundays I always served a brand-new hot meal that would extend through Monday and my husband's lunch.

Food had always been central to my family, so we kept up the tradition. One way or another, it would keep us together, right?

CHAPTER TWENTY

MOM IS WORKING...
AND THE KIDS ARE WATCHING

My PBS Years, 1989-2001

Starting in 1989, I worked at PBS, until the moment when I didn't.

The headquarters for the Public Broadcasting Service was located in these years on Braddock Place in Alexandria, Virginia. The organization served its over 350 member stations across the country with programming packages, as well as marketing and strategic branding initiatives.

I worked with the Creative Services arm on various advertising and promotion campaigns. I was the Go-To, I'll-Make-Your-Deadline, I'll-Nail-The-Budget Girl. That was my official role as Associate Director responsible for production supervision on marketing projects; non-stop pressure to perform. The demands were huge. And I was happy to accept them. How could I not be? It was exciting work, paid for with long hours. Hardly the framework for a traditional mother in a traditional role. Whatever my children thought of it, my husband must have felt conflicted.

On the one hand, it was great to have the extra income, a steady one at that.

On the other hand, the wife is not home to cook dinners. And, the wife spends a lot of time at work with co-workers. We had words about this. And, of course, when you're in the heat of being a young couple, you don't think about the long-term impact of harsh words shouted across a room. Or who's listening. Our parents had come from the generation of *"what goes on in the household, stays here."* Those generational habits got passed down; my husband and I made the same assumptions.

But again, being a young couple, you don't think about the impact of what you say...meant to be between husband and wife... and how those words affect the kids hearing them.

My kids were, and are, very mature. I've heard them say, "We love our parents." But, at certain points, they've been willing to admit, *our parents are not perfect.* Still, as a parent, it's better when you don't keep making the same mistakes. I certainly recognize my faults in the middle of all this, just from seeing our kids' reactions to particular situations. But what I've also seen in our children across the years is the ability to love people *where* they are. In fact, to know the true meaning of love. I believe what they witnessed between their father and me has had an impact on their expectations of love, as well as tolerance—to one extreme or the other. In their lives now, they may see red flags, but rather than make judgments, they wonder about how that individual could become a better person. They were raised in the church, so they have learned a few things about not judging, especially when the message came down that God loves everybody.

Yes, growing up, my kids were smart, and intuitive. But I believe we are products of our environment. So, these days, when I see how our behavior—particularly my own—might have impacted them, I say something.

It is certain that our kids were watching and listening, and that after decades of marriage, they knew the fabric of their family was ripped at the seams. They are now adults and they have their own opinions, but I do speak about the past when I find an opening. I try to send an encouraging word. And I use myself, not as a sacrificial lamb, but as an example. Because, after all these chapters of a life tested and tested again, I strongly believe that I have been one chosen by God to survive—and tell my story.

I believe I am now in the position to bless someone else.

~

Throughout our time together, my kids have been up close with my life's twists and turns. They've seen me struggling and they've seen me triumph. And during one very dramatic chapter, they saw me in the limelight. That's when I was a hard-driving production supervisor at PBS.

What an unexpected phenomenon to have your mom working among supremely gifted people busy producing programs that pull in a cache of Emmys and other accolades. I was working on big marketing and promotion initiatives, stage managing presentations at our national annual meeting of some 1200 attendees from member stations around the country, all the while meeting key people in our industry. And I mean truly great and well-known talents like Winton Marsalis, Shari Lewis, Fred Rogers, even Barney and the characters from Children's Television Workshop, the heroes of America's children.

I was especially fortunate to work with the singularly gifted mezzo-soprano, Denyce Graves, when our crew was in Leesburg producing a segment for Black History Month on PBS. I was helping with her makeup and she seemed interested in me. While we chatted, she asked about my background. I told an anecdote from my time in the Fine Arts School at Howard University when my professor, Dr. Norris, wanted me to consider opera as my major.

"Nope," I had said to him, "I want to sing R & B."

Denyce looked at me. "You didn't do opera? But you have the presence. You could have been one of the ones who paved the way for me. Did you know that I went to Howard? Dr. Norris was my professor!"

I was instantly reminded of a long-ago conversation with Dr. Norris.

"Opera," he had insisted, "… it's *you*, Cernata. "

Why could I never see those possibilities?

~

To get done everything that needed to be done on the PBS job, I had to fly all over the country. That meant time away from the kids. Certainly, they could see my hard work ethic and, sure, they could see pictures taken of me with the star talents of PBS all around the house. But was that a fair bargain for having a mom on the road?

What did they take from all of that?

I didn't realize it when I was in the middle of the grind—the circumstance that offered relief from a tense marriage—but it caused me to miss some of the big moments in my kids' lives. Like their birthdays. And graduations. I owe thanks to my father, Mom Louise and my nieces, who always supported and represented me on these occasions.

For example, my son—I'll never forget it—had received an award for outstanding achievement at his baccalaureate. But I wasn't there to applaud him; I was working on a show for PBS.

Another example: my youngest. The PBS annual meeting was always happening around her birthday; always scheduled for the same week of June. The year she turned ten, I wasn't there. And I didn't realize then its huge negative effect on her. I had tried to plan a great birthday for her in my absence. And it helped that I was very much a "community mom" arranging for pickups and drop-offs for all the kids who did sports. It built up enough good will for me to count on other community moms to pitch in when I was away. Or, I would order the pizza and cake for the birthday party and get someone else to pick it up when I couldn't.

But, that year, when my youngest child turned ten, she was particularly sad that Mommy wasn't there. That's when all the family and friends pitched in and planned a really special birthday party for her. Bless them all for being there, trying to fill in the gaps, including that time when my son got his award. They were there. Always. And sure enough, for this child's 10th birthday, I had ordered balloons and cake, and arranged all the other things you'd expect for such a big event, just as I always did.

But I wasn't going to be there. I would be at the annual meeting.

I realize now that I was in that crucial season as a parent when you are the essential element in the development of a young life. It was *that* important. And for all of us who struggle to balance life and work, I ask: what are we showing our children? With hindsight, I see the truth of that particular moment very clearly: it was more important for Mommy to be at home with her daughter than to stay an extra day at a very important meeting. I know this from the look on my daughter's face when I arrived at the country club pool to surprise her. I had come home in time---at least to attend *part* of the party. Late, but *there*. I'll never forget that moment.

For the other times, I have to ask myself: could I have cut my trip short, caught a red eye and flown home where I needed to be? Even an arrival in the middle of the night might have been appreciated. It was a fascinating, but conflicted, time in my life. The big wins, big losses. I have to wonder what the final tally was—or is.

I know how important having parents in your life is at critical times and key moments. Not just for a birthday. Once I helped produce a show in New York City, around my own birthday. I had planned to stay an extra two days to celebrate with my cousins in the city. But something was pulling at me. Even the creative director kept asking me to ride back to Washington, D.C. on the shuttle. She asked several times before I was convinced. I went back. Glad I did. When I returned to the house, my oldest daughter was sick—deathly sick. I scooped up the kids and rushed her to hospital. She had emergency surgery for a rupturing appendix. My daughter could have died. My decision to return turned out to be momentous. Thank heaven for good instincts.

Throughout my life there has been always a voice of reason that speaks to my heart. If I would just listen!

~

We worked very hard at the PBS annual meetings—everybody thinks it's all glitz and glamour. They see the results on TV, a show like *The Capital Fourth,* for example. But weeks before they begin, when you look behind-the-scenes of preparation for those meetings, you discover frantic activity over a long string of eleven and twelve-hour days. When I was the stage manager, a kind of production manager working with the Creative Director, it was a constant grind. Different technical teams at work—audio, video, all needing to be in synch. VPs running around making changes to the script. This was the life we lived: up all night rehearsing because we have President Bush coming in for a breakfast meeting. Working with the crew to make sure everybody is crystal clear on the coverage needed. Going over all the schematics. Over and over.

And I keep five little black outfits hanging on the rack in my room. (Black better achieves the invisibility required of stage crews.) One outfit for each day and repeat. I would lie across the bed for a moment's rest, then *rrrring,* the clock would go off. It's 4:30 am. Quick shower, grab one of those black outfits and run to the set.

It was—glorious? Maybe. But it was like, "Beat your face, Cernata. Wake up. Because you gotta be down there when the big guns need you."

So, I was living this life, saying, "I'm gonna work hard, I'm gonna be a VP someday. I can save money on the budget, I can negotiate." If this sounds in any way familiar, you have to stop and ask yourself, "What am I showing my kids?" I was running and chasing this dream. I thought I was showing my kids that hard work pays off. I wanted so badly for them to have the best of life. I knew, or I thought I knew, that because I had missed my opportunity to get my education, I had only this one shot to prove to all the managers who had given me an opportunity: I'm your girl, I can get it done. I can manage, I can produce, I have excellent people skills.

~

But every time I looked for a promotion, I would hit the wall, each time the message from Human Resources was clear. I didn't have the education. I didn't have the paper with the degree stamped on it. My supervisor, the print team's Creative Director, Anne Zangara, fought for me. She told me that producers were always coming up to her asking, "Where did you *find* her?"

But it didn't matter. No promotion. I found myself wondering what else I could do.

In March of 2001, the leadership at PBS changed. With that came new strategic priorities dictated by a tighter budget. Downsizing was in the wind. The staff had grown rather quickly, and now came the reckoning. After 9/11, it touched me. My layoff came as a derailment, but it wasn't a complete destruction. God was in there. And, apparently, I needed to be set down. Had I not been laid-off, I would still be grinding away with no good outcome. As it turned out, I faced a pivot point of enormous consequence.

My kids had watched everything that had been happening, through all the ups and downs. And they were very proud of me. Through it all, I'd wanted to keep them close. I was trying to shelter my kids as my mother did me. Same behavior. Taking care of everyone.

When my kids were teens, I watched them learning about relationships. Some blessed instinct told me I had to be transparent, as clear-sighted as possible with them. After all, they *were* watching. Children do watch, they emulate, they repeat. We've heard this. And you better believe it. So, I had to talk to them. There were moments when it was amusing, because they would slide up to me and say they needed to tell me something, but not to share it with the other ones. And I'd say ok. But then the next one would come in and reveal some piece of goings-on: "Well mom, I don't know if you know this, but this is what's happening…" (with the other one.) I smile as I remember, grateful that they trusted me enough to take me into their confidence.

They're grown now of course. All three of them, my son and my two daughters, show great maturity. I hear them now repeating some of the positive things I have poured into their lives all along. And I think, wow, *you really do listen to me*. And they'd be sure to say, *yeah mom, we listen to you*. They talk amongst themselves. And those are the things I have asked God for—to build a bond between them, that they may enjoy each other's company and be true brother and sisters until God calls them home. They are close. As I have prayed they would be, always there for each other.

Not surprisingly, there were some dark moments in my relationship with my children as a result of their father's and my destructive relationship. Emotions were high and there was plenty of judgment as I was blamed for it all. But my faith kept me anchored and, despite my feelings, I commanded respect and wouldn't tolerate anything less. It hurt me because, in all of those years, I had protected my children from everything. It was tricky for them, because they were hearing a lot from *his* perspective. But a very wise friend assured me, "One day Cernata, your children will rise up and call you blessed!"

CHAPTER TWENTY-ONE

NOW WHAT?

November, 2001

True, if it weren't for the layoffs I might still be in the grind. But I knew it was going to happen, because at some point before it actually did, I started giving away stuff. All the producers had given give me "swag", stuffed toys, etc. In the beginning of the year the new president had arrived and was instantly faced with reality. We'd grown. From a headquarter organization in one building with three-hundred-people to three buildings—and twice that many people—top-heavy with management. The stress had begun. There were in fact, three rounds of layoffs. During those months before 9/11, I remember the cold feeling in that building. PBS had been a family. I remember people coming in young, just out of college, and the way we shared life's big moments: the marriages, the building of families, all of it. We were close. Then, all of a sudden, they started getting rid of people.

Within two months...

I had hired someone from California; she got her apartment, got situated. She was loving it. Then I was told I had to let people go. And they told me that I had to let her go first. Concerned about my new hire, I went to consult with HR. No help was forthcoming. My hands were tied. I felt like I had ruined this young girl's life, ruined her chances at a great job at National Geographic, the one she'd given up for PBS

Meanwhile, I had started packing up my office. The only other people in the building might be some writers working late. And I was taking stuff to my car. Coming back upstairs, packing up and taking more stuff out to my car. Or giving it away.

When I got the guy in the print shop to take some of it, he said, "They are not going to get rid of *you*...they are *not.*" And I said, "It's gonna happen."

~

And so, the day it does happen, I am not caught by surprise. I walk into HR and among the people gathered there is Beth Wolfe, a colleague I had been working with for seven years prior to this point. She'd become a best friend. She's in tears, uncomprehending.

"How could this happen," she says. She knows how hard I've worked. She says the only thing standing in the way of my becoming a very successful executive...is the degree. "Not having one is something they will always throw back in to your face."

HR told me I was being laid off. They gave me the spiel: they were going to give me a few days to say goodbye to everyone. I stand and start to leave the room. I turn back once to look at them and say, "There will be no need for that. I'm going to go downstairs. I'm going to get my purse...I'll turn in my badge when I leave. And I'm gone."

"Well, what about your office," they ask.

"My office is already packed."

They are shocked.

CHAPTER TWENTY-TWO

DESTINY MAKES A PHONE CALL

December, 2001

God has always been instrumental in showing me my next move. For every new step I took, the groundwork was already laid. He never failed to indicate a way forward. When I lost the PBS job, I thought all hope was gone. But it happened for a good reason and by God's grace. He had to get me in a place where it was just him and me. Where I could depend on no one else.

~

After the layoff, it gets very tense in the home. My husband and I are in the midst of building a big house. There are debts. Two vehicles. Our relationship switches from "on" to "off" and back. Money is tight. And money is always the home wrecker… right?

I keep busy: I clean the house, shop for groceries, do the laundry and invent special activities for the children. But now everything is dependent upon my husband's income. And, we are *not* in a good relationship.

One day he says, "You need to get a job. Go apply to McDonalds…or are you too good for that?" We're talking about 2001. We are on the brink of massive changes in the job search sphere. Back in the day I could walk up to someone with my resumé and ask to speak to someone in HR. But now, after 9/11, our world has become a virtual society. All of a sudden no one is walking into any building and handing anyone anything. Everything has to be done online. And it takes hours. I get up just like I am going to work every morning and start filling out applications. It takes me all day to get through applying for two or three jobs. And when I'm not filling out applications, I'm struggling to figure out how many bills my unemployment check is going to pay.

But here I am one morning, at home, lying across the bed in tears, when the phone rings. It is the principal of the local high school. He says he has heard I'd been caught up in the PBS layoffs.

"I've watched you as a mom, I've watched you in public speaking forums. Ms. Morse, I have grant money and I need a voice for the community."

~

And that was the beginning of my long walk into purpose and destiny, starting with a job at the local high school, earning, maybe, fifteen dollars an hour, and scheduled to work seventeen hours a week. But because I am who I am, I took the job. My kids saw that. And you talk about a humbling experience? It was humbling. You go from being around award-winning writers and producers of Emmy-winning television shows…to working in the county as a public liaison. And making, what? A third of what you'd been making?

But I didn't focus on that. Because this was when things started to bloom in my mind and in my spirit. I saw a need to help these young people, to help the community bridge a gap toward understanding. The times needed understanding. In fact, the school system, now on its fourth demographic integration, could use all the understanding they could muster. You had the wealthiest of the wealthy from the Mount Vernon area while redistricting lines forced students from other, very different, backgrounds into the same school.

I became the voice of the school, building bridges and networking, getting local businesses involved to take ownership in their community and pour themselves into the school with whatever they had to give. By the time it was over, I'd had a seven-year run of being one of the best— they call it "parent liaison"—a kind of PR person. And that's when late one night, the principal, Dr. Henry Johnson, came to talk to me. The conversation turned out to be life-changing.

And may I pause to note, again, my kids were watching? My son was getting ready to graduate, but my oldest daughter was still at the school. (And of course when that job started, she was thinking, *oh no, mom's going to be working at the school!* until she eventually realized, *wow! My mom is the voice of the school.*) Remember, these were her teenage years and things were a little tough. She had witnessed all of the friction in the household and she was a daddy's girl. She fell in love and both her dad and I were not pleased. (Did she fall in love with a "good person, bad relationship choice" because of her parents? We'll see.)

In my new job, somewhere down deep, I may still have felt cast down and deeply humbled. It irked a bit. You go from working with high-profile personalities to being a public-school employee at one-third the pay. But when I looked at it from a different angle and saw the possibility of helping students, I felt my spirit bloom. And that lasted for a good seven years. In addition to being the parent liaison, I ran a newsletter. I was always in the local paper; I got noticed by the school board. It just evolved into a powerhouse position where I was actually changing young peoples' lives.

~

Here we are with Dr. Johnson, who has just walked into my little office to start that life-changing conversation.

"Ms. Morse, let me ask you something. What do you intend to do with your life?"

"I really don't know."

I'd received an offer from a local public broadcasting station in California—KCET. The guy was encouraging. "Cernata, we'll hire you in a heartbeat."

But I couldn't convince my husband to pack up and go to California. Which hurt, since I really wanted to go and needed to go. I loved television; I felt it was my calling.

Still, here's Dr. Johnson right in front of me saying how much I can contribute in a different way.

"You were meant to have a voice in this world. You have the presence, the looks, the gift of public speaking."

And all I can think about is my size, and all my other shortcomings of legend, pointed out to me over the years.

I hear myself saying, "Dr. Johnson, I can barely keep my head up with all I've been through."

He comes back, "But that's what makes you a diamond in the rough. God has given it all to you. Your voice. Your presence…look at you, you get noticed! But you need your education."

Another nudge comes from one of my other colleagues. He and I are monitoring a high school game. It's Homecoming. Coach Woods (now Dr. Michael Woods) and I are standing in front of the gym. My life is falling apart everywhere I look. But I had to put on a good show, complete with an upbeat outlook for myself and the kids. After all, "What would people think?"

This would be the second person in weeks who has challenged me to think about myself and my future for once in my life. I immediately thought about my kids; I am in no position to change my path. In fact, I was ready to cave in. Until a new Cernata spoke up. (And where did *she* come from!) "You have to do this now! It will benefit your entire family!"

Remember who's watching.

So, I come home with my marriage splitting at the seams, one thought turning in my head: *I have opened a door and, if I don't walk through it right now, it will close.*

Though I know my youngest, my daughter, will be the hardest hit, I also know that I have to do this for all of us.

I "walk through the door" and say: "I have an announcement to make. I am not going to be the hands-on mom anymore…cooking and cleaning and reminding you to go to practice. I've made a decision."

~

When I "walked through that door" my sole intention was going back to school to finish my Bachelor's degree. It was January, 2004. And that was exactly what I did.

My end goal was to work in public television again. But little did I know what would actually come to pass. Still watching, the kids would see that even with adversity blocking my way, a new path, unexpected, would unfold.

In fact, a restart in public television did not happen. Instead, I moved with Dr. Johnson from Fairfax County to the Montgomery County schools. His available funding could handle a position as school secretary. O.K. Now I've moved from PBS producer to school secretary. Could I have predicted that?

Yet my role was so much more! I worked side-by-side with Dr. Johnson to hire and build the staff in the reopening of the school. I was able to assist with developing process, even managing and developing the creative logo and design of the school.

Yes, I'd moved from a PBS producer to a school secretary. Yes, I'd been humbled by that. But you can't look at "man's titles." I walked into that opportunity, staying in touch with my children and guiding them on their path, while explaining mine. I'd say, "you all can cook, you can clean, you can learn to take care of yourselves."

Meanwhile, I learned that whatever position you have, you work hard, you do your best. And see what happens next. (It might be shaping you in ways you can't predict.)

The principal, my boss, would tell you that I actually helped run the school, taking up the challenges of doing things that hadn't been done before. Always drawn to theatre and the creativity it required, I wrote the script for the school's first play in an attempt at bridge-building, since integration was moving fast into that school system as well. A story about the play was published on the front page of the Silver Spring paper.

I worked hard. Finished my Bachelor's in 2006. And that's where I met my next mentor—Dr. Walter McCollum—who stepped in with a further challenge.

"Cernata, what are you going to do with your life?" Which quickly became, "You mean you're NOT going to pursue your Master's?"

"Absolutely not," I said. "I'm too old."

I was, at that point, in my late forties. But like any great negotiator, Dr. McCollum knew how to close. He did it by showing me the level of education he had in mind. I have to give him credit for his tactics. He was on message, and relentless: "You cannot tell me you can't do this."

Indeed, Dr. McCollum was a master strategist: he sent me to observe some of his classes. I went to lectures. Then took more classes. All the while, I'm sharing what I'm learning with my kids.

"Opportunity! You need to be around like-minded people, to surround yourself with stimulus!" This was academia. And I loved it.

After the shock of my not being "mom on duty' my kids actually became proud of me. They saw me soar in my studies and they even got the chance to step in and help with subjects where I actually needed their assistance. Imagine that...

My doubts were falling away, while my thoughts were clearing. I can do this. Even with my marriage falling apart, I knew. I can do this. I can stay up all hours of the night to study. I can survive the confrontations with my husband—which arise more often than before because he is not invested in this "going back to school" idea. But, despite all the roadblocks that will inevitably show up, I've made up my mind.

Even so, it's a time of reckoning. The stresses on the marriage will increase.

I'll have to keep my heart open to find new sources of strength; I'll have to keep my eyes on the prize.

Because the help from my father is there no longer.

CHAPTER TWENTY-THREE

MR. PETE

Flashback, c. 1984. In The ICU

My father was born in 1922 with an enlarged heart. His doctors determined that he would not live beyond the age of seven. He lived to the age of seventy-one.

Dad had been self-medicating with alcohol for some time. But around 1984, his day of reckoning was inching closer. Perhaps his decision had been awhile in the making, but it became a reality during an extraordinary, possibly "near death "experience in an intensive care unit, after yet another heart attack. I am in the middle of my second pregnancy, in the room, listening to the doctors recommend an operation.

"Mr. Stanton, your heart is expanding, we have to do something to stop it."

He will not entertain the idea. Once the doctors leave, this scene unfolds:

I am alone with him, keeping watch. He wakes up.

"What are you doing here?"

"Watching you." I say, "Dad, what's going on?

"My old ticker ain't working so good."

"Well, it ain't gonna work if every time you feel like a little drink, you take one."

The mood in the room shifts.

I hear him speak under his breath, "I have got to change my life."

He starts pulling out the many tubes connected to his body. Hysterical beeping starts as the machines respond: Emergency! Emergency!

Meanwhile, I see him carefully remove all the monitors attached to him, one by one, until he is free of them all. He kneels on the floor and begins to pray. I hear him, quite clearly, ask God to heal his body and remove his desire to taste alcohol.

With chaos swirling around him, he is serene. I can't believe what I am seeing as the nurses, alarmed by the rapidfire flicking of warning lights and screaming monitors, rush into his room to help him back onto the bed. They reconnect him.

Which is fine with him; he's finished his prayer.

~

I'm telling you, from the day he left outta that hospital, he was a changed man. So changed that, sometimes, I had to ask: "Where did *this* man come from?" Now, all he wanted was peace and serenity in his family. This new man was on a mission, deploying a strategy of selective scolding at any of us who showed up in his sightlines.

He wanted my sister and me to fix our broken relationship.

"Y'all need to get this relationship together."

He wanted my husband and me to stop fussing…and all the rest.

"Cernata, you know you can't do evil for evil."

"But Dad…" I'd say.

"Let it go. Be patient. At the end, God will wash it all out."

He had changed from the inside out as surely as a serpent changes its skin. Our whole family was like, *"Whoa…"*

He didn't want any more to drink. He just stopped. Cold Turkey.

~

In fact, he had stopped one other time before my mother passed and she was thrilled beyond belief. But her death triggered in him many years of grief and drinking was the way he coped.

~

Once he beat alcohol and turned his life around, Mr. Pete gave his family the gift of his clear and steady presence among us. We had over a decade of living with a man transformed—this was the best time of all we spent together, and for me, of having my daddy back in my life.

But he had one more thing to do before he died. A decade later, in his last days, he extracted a promise from me and my husband that we would work to keep our marriage vows and stay together for the sake of our kids. He was convinced that we both had much to offer as a couple. He cautioned us that if we kept our heads straight—and kept others out of our marriage—we'd be o.k. Perhaps it was advice from another era, because when two people are in a toxic marriage, it might require a different kind of thinking. But he gave us what he felt in his heart, and we were obliged to lean in and listen.

~

April, 1994
The Messenger
It has been raining for a week. Now it has slowed to a kindly drizzle, with light bursting through the window where I sit in the hospital room at my father's bedside. We speak quietly. Though we both sense this will be our final dialogue, we are not in a rush. All the words that have passed between us over a lifetime are coming to a pause; there is little else we need to say.

He is ready to leave his body; it's been failing him recently, as his enlarged heart keeps getting bigger. He's ready to go. All of a sudden, I feel this warm pressure on my shoulder as if to say, *be still.*

Outside the window a hummingbird, busy and bright, is feeding, moving from flower to flower. Kept aloft by the whizzing of its wings, it breaks in and out of the rain-washed light, scattering color in joyous bursts of red, blue, and green. I watch it settle on a bloom in the brief moments when I'm not studying my father's face.

He stops speaking, watching me. He smiles, and I feel his grip weaken.

Something moves through me, and I bow my head and whisper, *"Daddy, I will miss you."* But I know he is gone. No one else is in the room, except perhaps…

I glance back at the window to find the hummingbird gone.

Dear God…What was that? Had the tiny creature appeared just in time to scatter light along his path…was it a message?*…that heaven awaited…?*

I stay with him a while. I'm very calm. I wash his face and lift him ever so slightly so he rests a little higher on his pillows. I fold the covers neatly under his chest, then tidy the bed. I cross his hands in a gesture of repose. He's ready to meet the nurses and the doctor when I push the button for them to come. They rush into the room to get on with the administrative tasks, to note the time, to pronounce him dead. Others come in. Friends and family. Some weep, some wail. My distraught husband falls to his knees.

While I sit and wonder what just happened. *That bird.*

~

That year, in 1994, when my father extracted the promise from my husband and me that we would keep our marriage together, I was still at PBS, under pressure to perform. And it was true that my husband and I did not want to have anyone else raise our kids. We toughed it out.

Did we keep our promise to my father?

You know, at first, I tried. How could I gainsay a promise made to the father who died holding my hand? Through most of the following years, I did struggle to stay in the marriage for the sake of the kids.

But the tattering and tearing continued as other things started laying up in our relationship…like the outsiders. Other people were stepping into the marriage—on both our parts. That's how *we* allowed Satan to step in. (This is my assessment.) We were so miserable that it spilled over at work. Or church. I'd go with the kids alone to church; I'd feel like a single mom much of the time because he was working, often at night. There would be outbursts, moments of violence that became habitual and out of control. We went to counseling so many times, once with an older minister who advised my husband to take the kids to raise by himself and put me out of the house. Old school. Lord have mercy.

But I ask myself again, how did I—as with my first relationship—always get involved with people who compounded my low self-esteem?

Looking back, I believe my husband and I shared the same goals and dreams but the ways we meant to get there were different. That led to arguments. And, truth be told, our arguments would tend to escalate because I didn't have the female nurturing I needed to help me find words that would tamp the anger down. If he threw some remark my way, I couldn't resist the urge to retaliate. I was very likely to speak with violence in my voice, with cutting words that would prove my husband right: "Cernata has a sharp tongue!"

Moving forward, to the wiser person who lives in me now, this person knows to leave it up to God to do her vengeance. I look back with sadness to those days when I was still in survivor mode, taking matters into my own hands. As in, "If you hurt me, I'm gonna show you how it feels." But that strategy is a trickery of Satan and it runs in a vicious cycle. I've learned to be wary.

As I hope you're beginning to see as you travel this journey with me, this is a story told from my wisdom age, with the full benefit of insight delivered with God's impeccable timing.

CHAPTER TWENTY-FOUR

THE FABRIC WILL HOLD

Somehow, out of the fabric of a fraying marriage, my husband and I made good kids. Yes, we did, we made good kids. How, after all? Because both he and I are good people and we made our children of whole cloth despite our faults. They are of the fabric that holds. It may be pulled and stretched out of shape occasionally, but it will hold. My three children are each a wonder. And each of them has stepped in when I needed help. They've been essential to keeping me moving forward on my journey.

Their father was a phenomenal parent. I could never take that away from him. He was the best father any kid could ever have. He sacrificed his entire life for his children so that they might have the life he was never afforded. Now some might ask: "Well, how can any of that be true if the kids saw their mother being mistreated?" And though that did happen—it is a true statement—I put it behind me. I knew I could survive. There were also times when their father earned their disrespect. A vicious cycle tearing at us all.

Of course our children have been affected by the things they witnessed: the thorny dialogues and not-so-good engagements between my husband and me. Then came the divorce itself, and its fallout. Through it all they would ask questions like: how do you deal with new relationships? How do you talk to the other person? How do you manage an ongoing relationship? I was even asked "Mom why did you stay with Dad so long if you were unhappy?" Good question. Was it just because of the kids or was it something else? Something to ponder.

I've spent time with them, one by one, with advice—not about what their dad did, they can understand that better now that they're grown—but what I did wrong, and what I could advise them not to do to avoid going down the same road I did. God has blessed me, because now I can talk about all that happened in that marriage without holding my head down. That's key.

I've told them that, in a moment of insight, I let go of the mindset that had held me captive most of my life. I'd arrived at the point where, finally, I didn't care about what others thought of me. I told them I cared only about two things. "How am I living my life?" And "What am I doing to please God?"

With that insight in hand I became more open. For so long I was ashamed of stuff in my past, of what I had come from. It stood in such contrast to my husband's family, presenting the picture of a very wholesome country family. They were just "thick," meaning they did everything together, lived together, ate together, fought together. By contrast I came from a good family that had been forced to live through a cataclysmic history. In the beginning our family were very close-knit and wholesome too, but all hell broke loose after my mother died. It's been a lot to deal with, and it may have closed me down at times to the power of possibility.

But finally, I've started opening up. I'm telling my story. It's mine, warts and all, and I'm sharing it to help others avoid making the same mistakes—opening doors that nobody wants to open.

~

Given the strength of his intuition, my son could see the moment when divorce was coming. He saw it sooner than the girls did because he was older and that much wiser. He was able to see it wasn't all one person's fault. And now he can see how far I've come and how much I've accomplished since I left the marriage. It feels surreal. God let me fall out of the very bottom of the earth; I lost everything. Looked at on the surface, it appears that I did lose everything…my home and family, the home we had built and remodeled, the home that housed a marriage that appeared to be a cornerstone of the community.

Looking deeper, we see transformation.

CHAPTER TWENTY-FIVE

SMALL HANDS

2009

It was a landmark year. The list of signifying events is long.

Encouraged by my mentor, I began to prepare for my doctorate.

I had my first hip surgery.

My marriage was coming to an end, though I had tried to hold on for dear life. One last episode of extreme violence, when my life was threatened, clearly took "holding on" off the table.

The remnants of the Morse family were facing the loss of our home.

I had been working in government and, for the first time, I'd started to make a really nice salary, only to be laid off again.

We experienced the strange death of a family member, and were left to wonder what really happened, and why?

It all came crashing down, all the way down, to the point where you wonder: why not just stay here on the bottom? It might be easier. Nice and quiet. Simpler. Even comforting.

But *"Behold, new things have come."*

~

From the moment we separated and my husband left our home, never to return, we got new names. We were "exes." Ex-husband and ex-wife. I was left with the task of making the home we had shared affordable, so that those of us still living there could stay in it. But in 2009, the market was volatile, spiraling every which way. I launched an attempt to secure a favorable refinance program, along with that much-needed hip replacement, all in thirty days. I was able to make it through the initial period of the refinance program when you're faced with creating a payment plan. But, inevitably, the program needed to verify employment, something that couldn't happen because I was jobless. Grim as it was, I truly believe God allowed this to happen, as always, with impeccable timing.

And, as ever, there was a part of me that just kept moving my feet forward. One long stride at a time. Pacing, pacing. Doing and doing. Not giving up.

See "Cernata The Warrior".

But it was a miserable battle. A real slog. Our family home needed many repairs to make it livable, much less to make it sellable. The sump pump was not working. I had to replace the hot water heater. My two oldest kids and a grandson were living with me. The kids would say, "Ma, let it go." But I just didn't want to, thinking, maybe the ex and I can get together and make it right.

But it starts getting ugly. A bad scene from a B-movie.

Just watch...

The real estate agent is saying, "This is the time. We've got a solid buyer."

But my ex won't sign the papers.

The agent is saying, "You're going to lose it."

It is a beautiful house. To be exact, it is eighty-thousand-dollars-worth-of-remodeling beautiful. I'm hoping my "Ex" will see reason. This house is, after all, a combination of both our efforts. Can't he see we are set to lose it all?

Does he? No. He lets it go down.

~

There was a pivotal moment in this dark time where I knew I had lost everything—*again*. I saw only shadows. One day, I was sitting in the bedroom, my back turned away from the door, asking God to take me. I was tired, thinking, *"God, just come get me."* I wasn't planning to do any harm to myself, but…the thought was insistent…*my life insurance is three times my salary.* I bent over my knees, begging God to come get me. All of a sudden, behind me, I hear little feet padding toward me. It's my two-and-a-half-year-old grandson.

Now standing in front of me, he says, "Nana what you doing?" And he wipes the tears from my face. He says, "Nana, I love you, God loves you, don't cry. It's going to be all right." His mother calls out to him. And he runs back to the family room.

When those little hands touched my face, and he said, "I love you, Nana" I saw the light. All shadows disappeared. When he left the room, I said, "God give me strength." I thought, this is our next generation. And I knew right then I couldn't give up. Something kicked in. I didn't know where I was going or how I was going to make it through, but I heard these words, and the promise in them:

"I say to you, if you have faith like a grain of mustard seed…"

I dug in.

It was at a time when I was getting hit from all sides. Couldn't get hired, recovering from surgery… there were challenges everywhere I looked. You know, *The Enemy* likes to conjure up doubts in your spirit. *The Enemy* is a great accuser. I tell young people, "He will trick us. We will fall. Then he sits back. And then he accuses. But if we know God's promises and hide them in our heart, then we can say out loud, "God, you promised me that you will carry me through the storm." And I "done had aplenty of storms," as our old folk say. Every one of those storms helped me see more clearly that I am not perfect. But I know without a shadow of a doubt that God has carried me through every one of them. I can sense the presence of a fine carpenter shaping my life.

It is 2018 as I write this. And the last five years have been amazing. God knows that I know that he lives. I've been tested and tried. But, mark this, along the way I was promised I would build a house from the ground up.

How did that happen? First with an unwelcome revelation. In 2010, as I wrapped up things in our old home, and faced the need to find a new one, I realized that, all along, my "ex" had employed a clever strategy during our house negotiations. He knew me well. He knew that family and home and my kids meant everything to me. He reckoned if it all fell down, if he pressured me enough, if he held out long enough refusing to sell, that I would change. Maybe I'd act more like the traditional wife he'd wanted all along?

That didn't happen because our situation continued to be complicated by the "other" we were each seeing. He had somebody and I had somebody. It was messy. But it was also clear to me that the long chapter of our marriage had reached its last paragraph, its last sentence, its last punctuation mark. Full stop.

~

Look at this woman, Cernata, trying to survive. 50+ years old. Been with one man more than twenty-five years. Now she has to go back out into industry and society and find her new place in it. But first, more practically, she has to find a place to live, because this woman has been forced from the home that has sheltered her, for better and worse, through twenty-five years of marriage.

I knew that finding a place to live would not be easy. We'd gotten married in "old school" times, meaning all of our property, our goods, everything, were in his name. His first, mine second. This complicated my search. But a threatened animal has few thoughts in its head but safety. I was that harassed creature. I just wanted to live in a safe place.

When it all broke to pieces and scattered to the winds, I left that home even as the question persisted: "How am I going to make it on my own?"

But there was a purity in the situation. It was the first time in my life when I could say, "It's just me and God, and I don't have to depend on anyone else to provide my financial support.

Things started to turn.

CHAPTER TWENTY-SIX

THE APARTMENT

2010. Kingstowne, Va

I had to dig deep to appreciate what God had done for me, because there were moments in my bid for independence, especially at first, when it seemed as if my life was reeling backward, while lurching forward. Going to court to start the divorce process. Finding a new home. Finding work.

Questions swarmed around me in their usual fashion: What would people think of this prominent neighborhood family headed for a breakup? Gossiping and whispering buzzed like the plague of locusts in the Bible story.

I'd been betrayed by my home church of fifty-two years, where generations of our family had worshipped since the 30s. Where I had sung in multiple choirs and worked hard in many ministries. But the one time I reached out for help, they didn't come. Instead, gossip, lively as could be, made the rounds. And who else came around? The Deacons, eager to give me a dressing down. And the irony was, I'd been at that church long before any of them were. But that didn't stop them from asking me, "Why are you in the predicament you're in? Where's your husband?"

My sense of betrayal was now full and complete. I could only conclude that church is a place of sinners. Saints don't need it. And I thought, if I can't go in to the House of the Lord and ask for help, where can I go?

The answer came to me…but not from the church deacons!'

"Your friends may betray you; others may desert you, but I will always be here."

God spoke with impeccable timing and clear purpose. I got the message. And I stepped out on faith.

~

I'd been brought to my knees when I found myself engaged in this dialogue.

"God, I don't know where I'm going next, or what I'm doing. I've got to move out of my home and into somewhere new, but I don't have the money to afford a nice place, much less a safe one."

Take what you have and go to this area where you want to live, and go in and talk to the manager."

"That manager's not going to let me in!"

"Go."

The rent was $1800 a month. And you had to pay two months in advance on deposit. I had $1500. That was all I had.

But I went in to the manager's office praying under my breath, God you've gotta help me, you've gotta make this happen. There I was, praying away, because there was no home to go back to; we were heading into foreclosure.

The manager looked at me while I told her my story. She said, "You know Ms. Morse, I'm going to help you. I feel like helping somebody today."

I wanted to cry.

She said, "You give me one thousand dollars, and keep the rest. I've got an apartment that I need to rent and it's in a great building. You've got some good neighbors who've been there since the complex opened, some older folks, some young people. A nice mix. It's a good building."

I said, "You're serious?"

"I'm going to give you the keys, go see if you like it."

And when I walked into that apartment I breathed out.

"Oh my God!"

It was a roommate-type arrangement, so my oldest daughter and my grandson could have one of the bedrooms and a bathroom for privacy. I'd have the other. We'd have what we needed, with even an office space for me. And a little balcony.

And, you know what? I felt safe there.

She took the thousand dollars, and that left me five-hundred to move.

Nobody believes that story.

But God did it.

CHAPTER TWENTY-SEVEN

RULER OF MANY THINGS

I moved into the apartment, but I didn't unpack any boxes. I was moping around, in a bad mood. What was going on with me?

After all I went through to get it, I was actually angry to be in this apartment in Kingstowne, Virginia. Who knew what I was thinking?

And then came the message, as clear as the nose on my face:

"If you don't appreciate what I give you now, how can you be the ruler of many things?"

I straightened up quick. "Lord, thank you for a roof over my head, and my daughter's and my grandson's."

In the next forty-eight hours I had unpacked all of those boxes. I was ready for my oldest daughter to walk through the door to the aromas of a home-cooked meal. She looked around. Sniffed. Ten minutes later I heard her on the phone with one of her siblings: "I don't know what's going on, but it smells like Thanksgiving in here. The boxes are unpacked, there are pictures on the wall, and we're moved in."

~

I was in that apartment for four years. And God dealt with me in many ways. He used my middle child, my oldest daughter, to teach me. "Mommy, I didn't realize everything you were going through when I was a child…" she'd say. Bless her. It was only during our time living together that we could walk through the past and get free of some misunderstanding. At one point, I had wanted her to go in a different direction. There was a rift. But God had a plan. Who knows what would have happened without her son, that sweet child, in my life? (Oh, he of the small hands.) My daughter needed to be back home from college to become a mother. And it was two years later that her child would comfort me and lighten my days from that time forward. The other two kids were off building their lives: my son Zack out on his own, and my youngest daughter, Zelexis getting her degree. In that apartment at that time it was simply the three of us, my daughter, her son and me, living through new chapters. She witnessed my anguish as I struggled to shape a life that would make a difference in this world. These kids of mine do see what I've been able to overcome in order to have an impact.

I am grateful. Lord, I am fortunate.

CHAPTER TWENTY-EIGHT

AMONG THE STARS

2010

Another year of great transition. Ready…or not? Apparently it doesn't matter, because destiny is on the move.

To understand its impact we need to roll back a bit to the moment when I had finished my Master's in 2009, and my graduate study mentor, Dr. Walter McCollum pops up with a new idea.

"Now…" he says, "what'cha gonna do?"

"I think I'm going for the gold."

We've been talking for a while about this, back and forth, to do it or not. The PhD

"I never would have believed you've experienced all you have in such a short lifetime," he says, upon hearing more details of my long twisting, story. "Going for the gold?" he says. "Get the PhD Then publish, get the credibility you deserve."

Interesting he would say that because I'd already been encouraged to go down the publishing path in a late-night phone conversation with my girlfriend. I was home alone, while my husband was working. Or, at least, out of the house.

My girlfriend says, "You got a story to tell."

And I reply, "Girl, I can't do that. Everybody'd think I'm crazy."

She insists. "It's going to rock this world."

Stranger still, she wasn't the only one to prod me in this direction; one of the writers at PBS came up to me and told me she'd had a dream about me.

"What kind of dream?"

"I dreamt that you were in a public forum speaking to an enormous crowd, and they were all clapping and crying."

"Clapping AND crying, what in the *world?*"

"I saw it," she says.

~

Sure enough, in 2010, I started my doctorate. I graduated in 2014 from Walden University with a 4.0. Now I am an adjunct professor at multiple online universities and have recently started in the position of Dissertation Chair, at the University of Phoenix, where there is now a waiting list of students interested in working with me. Most recently, I've accepted a position as Doctoral Mentor at Capella University. Things have come a long way because of those who believed in me and urged me up the ladder of learning.

Yet there is more to tell of the journey that brought me here, of the people whose hearts and hands helped God do his work, transforming me into an educated woman with a purpose.

On to that story: let's adjust the lens. And reset our time code…

Do you recall the incident when I thought I had lost my opportunity to go to school?. I remember my godmother saying, "You will be blessed beyond measure". I remind my younger daughter, "Remember you saw what God has done in my life. And that's why these things have happened to me, so that you all could see." I think of my grandson and his small hands on my face. I also believe God is no respecter of persons; if he did this for me, he will do this for anyone. I like this quote from the video personality, Donnie Simpson: "Reach for the moon, and if you miss, you'll be among the stars."

And still, we must talk about storms and their heavenly follow up, when clouds part and the sun breaks through.

~

TIME CODE: 2004. This was the year, you'll remember, when I had walked through the door to our house with an announcement for my family: "I'm going back to school." Now I was poised to show up in class and was again plagued by my old enemy. Doubt. "What will people say, will they see me as old? Will I fit in? And the worry about my kids. My eldest two were away at college, but what about the impact of all this on my youngest, still in high school?

I'd been stoked for this moment by my mentors in the two high schools where I'd worked as a student advocate and parent liaison. I had commanded a presence, begun to find my voice as an advocate, speaking for at-risk youth. In fact, that work had become a burning passion. But I agreed with all my mentors: I needed more educational credentials for my voice to be heard and taken seriously. I knew I had to get those degrees. And my colleagues had gone so far as to insist: this was the time to be selfish, to do this for myself, because in the long run it would benefit my family as well.

~

It is the first day of school, at the University of Phoenix. I'm in the course room in Mark Center, in a hotel. It isn't a traditional classroom, more like a business environment, a kind of conference room, u-shaped, with media setups dispersed throughout. I glance around the room and see to my surprise, a cross-pollination of America. We begin the introductions and I realize, as one after the other shares a brief bio, that we are in a space of enormous diversity. Young, old, blue, black, white, and every shade of brown; there is diversity every which way you look at it, but one thing we hold in common: we're *all* coming back for a second chance.

And I see the beauty in that. The sense of difference between me and them fades away. I am not the "old" one. And I don't just "fit it," I am in my element. I even have something of value to offer my fellow students. It's my experience! My experience working in television production and all that I gathered later in organizations and in business. I can offer insights into ways of doing, being and working in worlds beyond the classroom. I have something my fellow students want! Meanwhile, I could only look on in awe at how quickly the younger students grasped the concepts.

We begin to work on a learning module system which means we must quickly adapt to its guidelines. To do this we call on what collaboration skills we find in that moment, building others as we go along. I find myself nominated as team leader in many modules we take on. I've found my niche! It isn't always easy, but I know I am where I'm meant to be.

~

My time as a student did take me away from my family, and I did not calculate the impact correctly. Still, we survived; my children and I are better for the effort I made to get advanced degrees. Because, only with those in hand, could I step into my destiny.

Was there a particular moment when that destiny came into focus for me? Indeed, thanks to a colleague at PBS, Millicent Massey, there was. I'd seen her as a public speaker and was amazed at her talent and effectiveness. Little did I know that Millicent had a vision for me.

One day she comes into my office at PBS. Says, "Whacha doin'?"

"I'm trying to put together a budget, I'm up against it."

But Millicent is eager to share her vision and gets on with it.

"I see how you collaborate, how well you work with people. But when you need to, you stand your ground. You've proved you have value. That brings you a certain amount of success here, but I have had a vision of you on a different platform."

I joke, "Well what have you eaten to give you heartburn?!"

Undeterred, Millicent launches her big idea. "I see you on stage. Speaking to a large forum of people. In my vision, I am backstage, just watching, watching my vision of you come true. You are going to be able to reach God's people."

"But Millicent," I say, "my story is so jacked up I can't even get myself to the water fountain."

Ms. Massey is fired up: "God is going to turn all your broken pieces into a masterpiece."

I'm breathless, no words come.

"God is going to use you. You're going to be a force to be reckoned with. When that day comes, it is my prayer that I will be able to see you walk in your destiny."

And with that, she hugs me, turns, and walks out of my office.

Yet when I first returned to school to complete my undergrad degree, I didn't remember that conversation. And given the demands of juggling family and work with school, I'd begun to doubt my ability to continue on after I got my Bachelor's. My epiphany came first after I'd completed it. Again, it was my mentor, Dr. McCollum, who challenged me. It was a well-timed prompt, but it took one more to blow the door open.

~

TIME CODE: 2006. We're at the graduation ceremony. I'll be receiving my Bachelor's. A classmate arrives late and I let her hop in front of me. That puts me in the last seat in my row, which will be the first seat to walk up to get a degree. From this seat I have a perfect view of the stage; my eyes are on our one PhD candidate. When she walks across the stage, she does it full on, with tears of joy, excitement, and an undeniable pride in her accomplishment. When the professor hoods her, she throws both hands up and bows her head. That does it. Something blooms in me. I think, that could be me.

From my lucky seat, I'm the first one to go up on stage and get my degree. After so many years of off and on, I've earned my Bachelor's.

After the ceremony, my mentor is back in my face, "Surely you're going to get your Master's." And not skipping a beat, "I want you to come to some of my lectures. I just want you to experience it."

And I do. I sit in those lectures, and watch. At the end of each lecture, he takes a break and comes back to ask, "What do you think?"

I say, "I could do that with my eyes closed." And he says, "You certainly can."

~

TIME CODE: 2008. I enrolled in the Master's program in less than a month. Got my degree in less than 18 months. (With a 3.9 grade point.) And just as I came close to fulfilling my course work in that program, Dr. McCollum then challenged me to consider going for a PhD.

This is a fast-moving story, isn't it? No sooner have I claimed my Master's when my mentor dangles that PhD carrot in front of me. Of course, by this time he knew my trajectory well enough: my from-the-bottom up-story with a few "bottomed outs" along the way. He had a similar story of his own and insisted, "God can do this for you. You'll have the platform and the credential to be what you need to be."

It reminded me of the conversation with Millicent Massey, and I brought up my idea of writing my story, which had been popping up in different conversations with many friends. Now, mind you, Ms. Massey is an accomplished media professional; I always pay attention to what she says.

Often as I lay in bed, dreaming, I thought about the idea of a book.

God had taught me I would have to walk through some difficulty to get to my destiny. But perhaps I was getting nearer to turning that journey into a story. I would need to step into it. There is a process, after all.

I was invited to a dinner with Dr. McCollum's PhD candidates. The men well outnumbered the women. I saw a cross-pollination of races but not gender. I looked at that wobbly ratio and said to myself, I need to consider this next step. In fact, the imbalance of women in the room triggered something bigger. I suspected I would eventually find my voice, but I was just as certain it would be a hard slog.

Indeed, four years of challenging events lay ahead, from 2008 until 2012:

My marriage would deteriorate to the point of separation.

I would lose my home.

And I would become deathly ill.

But the PhD journey would teach me that I too could be a Dean's List student. Again, I felt the door of opportunity open; I simply walked through it. I wasn't going to let fear stop me. I would walk by faith.

Walk by faith? Honestly, I found it difficult to soldier on. I was fighting a battle on several fronts: logistically, physically, emotionally and mentally. But I felt an urgency. This could be my breakthrough moment. If I could get this final, most powerful credential, I could finally gain complete financial independence from my spouse. And back in 2008, when the long slog started, that meant everything.

My mentor had shared the significant financial benefits of earning a PhD. Beyond that, the financial pivot would show my kids all that could be gained through further education. Not simply wealth, but sustainability; the chance to expand and grow the ways I could have a positive influence out there in the world. Could I find speaking opportunities? Could the PhD be a straightforward way to lend a hand to our kids, to support their success? Yes, of course. But to manage it all I had to focus; I had to let some things go, like social engagements and even my ministries at church.

~

Who encouraged me to stick it out? Our kids. All through the PhD journey, they saw the tears; they saw the times I fell across the bed and cried out, "I can't do this anymore; I think I've made a horrible mistake!" My oldest daughter was there for me, of course, because of our time living together for many years before she got married. She would come into my room and say, "Mom you've got to eat something." Or, stuff would come up and upset me and stall my efforts to do the needed research and writing on my assignments. But she would always encourage me, "Mom, you are going to be Dr. Morse."

Or my son would call and ask where I was; he hadn't heard from me lately. He'd say—and remember he's a guy— "Mom, it's just like pledging." That's my old soul, the wise one with the deep bass voice, who also came up with this gem: "I salute you, mom, you're going to be a beast when you get this done!"

It was the kids. It was *those kids!* Consistently, every day, they were my biggest champions. Then, it seemed like all at once the noise stopped. My oldest daughter headed off to Japan with her son to join her husband. My youngest daughter took up an apprenticeship with a dental practice in Greensboro. It was quiet all around me.

But at that point I was fortunate to have others step into the role of champion. In 2011, I met a man who would become a dear friend and supporter. Meeting Reverend Scofield was easy, lucky in more than one way. My daughter needed a car, and a friend found this particular salesman to supply it.

Little did we know, until we were well into the friendship, that he was also a Bishop from the Baltimore area. He is from a legacy of bishops and members of the cloth. As he came to know more about me, he became a "Chief Encourager" and advisor. He assured me that my life would not be in vain. When I started to flag, often simply too tired to put one foot in front of the other, he would prompt me to recommit and focus on the PhD. "The only thing standing between you and your degree is your doubt and fear. Do not give *The Enemy* that power."

Bishop Scofield was always my spiritual advisor and friend when I needed one most.

Right down to the last mile of my PhD track, there were dry spells, when the ground ahead would seem like a desert, hard-packed and unyielding. But, when I needed encouraging words, showers would come, and the path would clear.

CHAPTER TWENTY-NINE

2012

It is the year of my divorce; I am seriously ill. When the first symptoms start in 2010, it seems like food poisoning. There are various options offered up as reasons. Was it perhaps a botched surgery from earlier? There's nothing conclusive. It remains mysterious, while slithering from scary to scarier. Every three or four months I have to be rushed to the hospital, even when I'm far from home. Finally, I end up in the ER in Greensboro, North Carolina, while on a visit to my youngest daughter who is studying there. A few months later, it is obvious something is wrong. I can no longer ignore warnings my body had been sending over the previous two years. These latest, sudden, episodes land me in The Washington Hospital Center in D. C. in August, 2012. I undergo major abdominal surgery and spend seventeen days in the hospital recovering. It is touch and go for a while with, again, no certain prognosis.

As you have seen, my life has never been simple or straightforward so, in addition to worrying over my health, I'm still in graduate school studying for my PhD. To gain that long-sought prize has been my mainstay; it's given me purpose; held me together through all the demanding years that brought me to this moment. But now, my condition is considered so life-threatening that my significant other has come to join the others gathered at my bedside to watch and pray. My sister is here, as are my nieces and ex-husband who shows up to sit by my bed for two hours. He shares a simple message, "Cernata, you have so much to live for."

My youngest is at a significant point in her education in Greensboro but I think she should be spared the news that her mom is in a medical crisis. The other siblings don't agree. Once she's told, she shows up immediately.

"What are you doing here?!" I say, as if to send her back to class.

A born doctor, she gives me the look. "I'm here *checking* on you."

The doctors have told the family that if my body doesn't come around on its own, in other words, if it doesn't stop shutting down, there's nothing further they can do. I have a massive blockage in my intestine. Already the medical team has gone through a lot— procedure after procedure—to clear the situation, and are finally ready to be optimistic. They say we may be at an upturn. If only my body will do its part.

My body does come around. After spending time with me in the hospital, my oldest daughter leaves the country to be with her husband deployed overseas.

Back home in Kingstowne, grateful for the masterful skills of the surgeons, I know it is nothing but God's grace and mercy that's kept me. In fact, one day while in the hospital the Head Surgical Nurse comes to visit me in my room. I don't recognize her, but she smiles and asks how I am doing. I say, "I'm fighting for my life!"

She smiles again and says, "You will be fine." And tells me a story. "Because when you were under anesthesia you said, 'God, you kept me!' One of the interns was surprised by this, and asked if I'd been given the right amount of anesthesia. I said to them, 'she's o.k., that's just the spirit within her.'"

Now I'm home alone recuperating—with a *lot* of time to pray and think. I have my doctoral work to return to, which comes as a relief after so much time in a hospital bed.

In fact, it's the first time I've been totally by myself since I was in my early twenties. I become accustomed to it. It's during these days that I realize, once again, I can do anything with God by my side.

"I have been there, all the time."

There are a few more medical bumps in the road to clear, but I know I have help now. I'll move forward.

CHAPTER THIRTY

FROM THE GROUND UP

c. 2014, Ashburn, Va

Though I'd been able to stay in the apartment for four years, it was time to move again. Hit hard with a lot of taxes, I began to look for housing, focused on town houses I could afford. But the competition was steep. I would think I had found a possibility and someone would come in right behind me with a competitive bid or a willingness to pay cash. Finally, I found a town house. Though the house itself was perfect, the location was not. OK, but not perfect. I prayed about it.

"God show me where I need to move."

I made a bid for the town house and dove deep into the process until I was approved to buy. The seller was in the military; we worked out a good deal. Two days before the closing, I found a new job bumping my salary up by $25K—the most money I'd made in my life. But the hiring company only paid once a month. And the mortgage bank needed to see a record of two salary payments. Meanwhile my seller was getting ready to be deployed; she couldn't wait two more months. We did everything we could to save the contract. But the bank manager stood fast. "No." He wouldn't approve it, "Unless I see those two pay stubs." One minute I was buoyed by the good news of a new job with a big raise; the next minute the deal fell through. I was devastated.

Doubts had set in. I felt hopeless again, thinking maybe I'd made a mistake, maybe I wouldn't make it by myself. All this stuff was piling up in my head. Until...

~

It's a Sunday morning. As always, I go to church, and hear a sermon about faith. This time something new in the sermon strikes me. Then it starts to work its way right into my marrow. The preacher is talking about God's timing. "God's *impeccable* timing?" It was the first time I'd heard that phrase. Which of course I very much needed to hear just then. (And have every day since.)

Now I'm driving home, back from Washington, D. C. traveling south on I-395, when my oldest daughter calls. She's asking if I'm ok.

"Mama, I didn't hear you leave... what do you want for dinner?"

"I'm on my way home."

Long pause.

"Are you crying?!" she asks. "What's wrong?"

"I just came from church ... I'm tired. I don't know what else to do. I feel like I've tried and tried to do right ... but I just can't catch a break. I lost the contract for the house."

My daughter comes back in a split second. "Mom, I don't know why this is happening, or what's going on ... but God is going to bless you. He's going to set you down right in Northern Virginia, right in the middle of your family, where you all grew up ... I believe you're going to build a house from the ground up."

And I say, "You're crazy, I don't have that kind of money ..."

But when she says that part, *"I believe God is gonna set you down right where..."* I look up at the sign to check the name and number of the exit.

Where I was at that moment, that very exit, would become the turnoff to the new home that I would build and move into three years later. That ... very ... same ... exit.

We go on talking, with her repeating, "I believe you're going to build a house from the ground up."

I'm still in protest mode. "No way!"

But she's back. "Ma, I don't know how you're going to do it, but God's going to do it."

And when would that be? I'm thinking…*Not so fast, Cernata. God's impeccable timing is not necessarily predictable.*

~

Immediately a call comes in. This time it's my sister.

She asks in excitement, "Sis, are you ready to move?"

I respond in tears, telling her how I lost the contract.

Then she began to cry, saying, "Sis I don't know why all of this is happening to you, but I know God has a plan. You've been through so much and I'm going to keep praying for you.

I said, "I know, and thanks. But I'm just so distraught."

I'm thinking, *"This is my sister and she's praying for me."*

We hung up.

And I started to wait for whatever came next.

CHAPTER THIRTY-ONE

THE SWEET WAYS OF LOVE

Throughout my ups and downs, Mom Louise had been the mother figure in my life after my mother's death. Although my father never wanted anyone to take me from him, Mom Louise was destined to become a powerful persona in my life. She sheltered me in times of trouble, provided food and safe haven when I needed it, and brought a touch of normalcy to my life. But it wasn't just through hard times that she showed up and lent her grace, she was there throughout all our lives, and as time moved on, she celebrated the signature moments as well. Birthdays all around. Weddings. The birth of children. The passings on. And I now celebrate her. Thank you, Mom Louise.

She, like most of the elders in my life, loved my then husband and for good reason. He was a good man. Along with Mom Louise, I have to give him credit: he gave me a lifestyle I hadn't experienced until he came along, namely, one with stability. Yes, all the elders adored him and Mom Louise was no exception. It was a natural step to hire her as the babysitter for each of our children, a role she fully inhabited. Her spirit could fill a room, so we welcomed Mom Louise as the new and needed matriarch in our family.

My fondest memory of her might well be her monumental decision, finally—*finally*—to share with me her secret recipe for homemade pound cake. One Saturday she called me. It was time. I would be invested in the knowledge.

That investment began when I was introduced to several unique baking pans I hadn't seen anywhere before. Was this the secret she held, was this why she was the best pound cake maker in the neighborhood— and possibly the four counties north and south of us? Hmmm...she revealed her secrets and I vowed not to share them with anyone other than my daughters. (Sadly, this vow must include you, dear readers.) Thanks to Mom Louise I'm now known as the best pound cake baker around, here, there and anywhere. I claim it. I own it. I wear the crown. Now, as is fitting, my daughters also hold the keys to the recipe, having added their own touches. (We live in an era of customization, do we not, dear readers?)

Mom Louise, you'll never be forgotten, especially as we remember our last Christmas holiday together. You'll forever be in our hearts... especially those times when we lift our plates, politely, to beg, *please*, may I have another slice of pound cake?

CHAPTER THIRTY-TWO

I BUILD A HOUSE

November, 2014 to early 2015

It's now many months after my conversation with my oldest daughter, when she proposed to me that I would build a house from the ground up. She's still quite confident that this far-fetched idea will come to pass.

I'm at work. I get a phone call. My girlfriend on the other end of the line tells me to go to the nearest parking lot to take the call. It's bad. Our Mom Louise, the woman whose outsized talent for loving brought her often to our doorstep to patch up broken lives, has died. I pull into the parking lot and sit in the car. Mom Louise is gone and our whole family is weeping.

While I'm sitting in the car, my niece calls. (Mom Louise poured love into her life too.) Of course she's crying while she's talking to me and, in the middle of that, she asks, "Are you interested in our father's land?"

Startled, I say, *"What!"* Still feeling the pain of the news about Mom Louise, I'm barely able to parse what's going on. *Their father's land?*

To add further to the eeriness of the moment, I had in fact asked about that parcel of land, much earlier, when my nieces' father, my brother-in law, Roger, died. But that was the wrong time to ask anybody about it. And at the time my youngest niece very quickly brushed me off, saying no, no, no, her dad had made plans to do something else with it.

Shame on me. It was not the right time to pose that question. Bad timing.

But now, in the moment of this new phone call, the timing works differently, *impeccably*, because the nieces are getting ready to lose the land and need a solution. And they ask me: *Am I interested?*

We make a deal; I conducted business as if I was purchasing the land. The cornerstone is laid, the prophecy will be fulfilled. I will build a house from the ground up. And it will take over three years.

~

Of course all did not run smooth and easy. For one thing, I was pursued by aggressive, sometimes threatening developers wanting to get their hands on my land. Nor did the county give me a break. (You'd think they were set against me.) For what reason? Might they have had doubts about a single African-American woman's plans to build that big'a house all on her own?

When I'd take one step, they would push me back five. And every time I'd take ten steps, they would push me back twenty. So, I devised a strategy: I chose well-spoken white men to be my face and voice. It worked. And I prayed—every day—and right down through the minutiae of the banking and the financing process. It got hectic and I stayed frantic. Until this interesting thing happens...

When I go to pay off taxes on the land, I discover that someone has held it off the auction block until I get the financing to pay the taxes. Things again started to turn. True, the bank didn't lend me the money. But they had an investor. One of the bankers had done some research and gotten to know me, and let me know he had someone who might be able to help. And this gentleman, the investor, had already looked me up, done his research, and learned my story. Next step, I had to go meet him at Ashburn, Virginia, at a bank. I was very nervous because, of course, this man held my future in his grip. When I got there, he let me know that he had already made his decision, he just wanted to meet me and talk to me. He was ready to take a chance. He was prepared to lend me the money, saying I'm going to help you get this project started, which we did, though it was very hard.

For one thing, I couldn't find a builder.

Then, that same helpful banker introduced me to a young builder who had done million-dollar restoration work and remodeling—but had never built a house from the ground up. So, he and I sat down and talked. I told him about my dream house, how I wanted it laid out, this, that and the other. Obviously, God had put the pieces in place because this young builder took a chance on me and I took a chance on him. We built the house in about twelve months. But it was rough, because he was new to our county—came from another county in Virginia—so he was on a learning curve. But I'm telling you, talk about a lot of prayer, those last twelve to fourteen months pulled in a lot of prayer.

When he started taking the measure of the land, I would come out to the location and pray. I mean I would *pray*. I asked God to protect every inch of that property from the time of my being there through every generation to come, that no hurt, harm or danger, or destruction, or malice or hatred, would come to this place. My home would be a home of peace and refuge.

Then, when they began to erect the structure, I could not believe my eyes.

I had designed the house and had the blueprints to prove it, but when I saw it being built, coming to life with every piece of framing…oh…it was truly a gift from on high. Every single member of my family, everybody who knows me and my story knows it was God who built that house. It stands tall and stately, tucked back on a small private road, one that had started to get a bit rundown. But all of a sudden, from nothing, this house rose from the ground to be a beacon of light on that dark road.

These days, when I drive up to that house, I actually do see a light.

It's one I purchased—a chandelier. The design is called "Halo." When I saw it in Restoration Hardware, I said "Oh, my God, it's beautiful." (Very simple, but the crystal is absolutely beautiful, and it is in the shape of a halo. When it's turned on it glows.) When I saw it in the store, I wanted it right away. I could imagine everyone who walked into my home feeling its warmth the moment they entered. And I would feel that glow every time I would walk up my steps. When the builder was ready to hang the light, I asked him to hang it just so. "I didn't want it to be seen from the outside, because I didn't want to boast or brag, but I did want folks approaching to feel the warmth of that light." And that's exactly what he did.

As I tell you this story, I am sitting in my wonderful house, and…Bang! Plunk! one of my shelves comes off the wall in my big closet and dumps all my clothes on the floor. Is this a sign? Note that when I moved in, I gave away twenty bags of clothes. Imagine, the girl who came from nothing, giving away that many clothes. What would my mother, the supremely gifted dressmaker, think?

I'm in the house; it's a bit overwhelming. This is more house than I…well…I didn't know what I was designing, I just went for it.

Careful what you ask for?

But I see a certain glow in my youngest daughter's eyes when she walks in. Remember, when we moved, she was almost ripped from the home she grew up in. Now she has her own space to greet her when she comes home from school. She's home, and she thinks the house is beautiful. It's still in progress, because it takes time; it's a big project. But just to be able to accomplish this, a woman of my age, and a divorcée, is to say, "You can do anything. You have not finished your journey. You can do anything, when you put your mind to it."

This book too will be done, despite the distractions, despite *The Enemy's* feints and dodges as he tries to block me. It reaffirms to me that sharing my story is exactly what I should be doing.

But I want to remain humble. When I look at pictures of the house, of course I feel proud. Even my great nephew, grandson to Roger, gazing at the house, said: "My grandfather would be smiling."

It is very easy for The Human to become prideful, or boastful, and so I ask God to keep me humble. And never allow me to forget that I'm on a journey. This too is part of my journey, to build a home from the ground up. God allowed this.

I keep telling my kids, "God knows that I know he's a miracle worker. But I've got you, my wonderful kids, and you've seen every step of my journey in extreme close-up. At the time of this writing, my kids are 35, 33 and 29 years old and doing well, each on their own path. I've said to them, "You heard the arguments and the fighting, the back and forth, the accusations. You've seen me crying, you've seen me wailing. You've seen it all, you've heard it all. But you've also seen the other side of that journey."

And they do tell me that my commitment and dedication is to be admired... that I will be a lesson to others. And I say again to them, I want to leave a legacy for my younger generations, to say that if you remain faithful, you will be blessed, and you will prove that everything comes from God. I want to leave word that this journey is not going to be easy—it's a hard journey—but when you persevere God may use you as a testimony.

I'm overwhelmed when I see the house. Overwhelmed, because it is a testament: God thought enough of me to build me a house.

I'm telling you, seven years ago, eight years ago, I wouldn't have believed I'd be doing this. But God allowed a faith walk. Even down to the bank. Down to the wire. Because there was a moment when no bank would give me a loan. That kind investor did step up but he said—still kindly— "I'm not going to pull the trigger on the note." But he offered other help. Advice: "We have got to find a new bank."

So, I started calling around. I said, "God I know you would not bring me this far, just to walk out on me. I talked to yet another investor, and this one said, "You're from Alexandria. Why haven't you tried Burke

and Herbert? They're known for taking care of their own community."
I knew they liked to help people whose family had roots in the town.
So, I called the VP of mortgages. Who said, "Dr. Morse, we're going
to see… can we help you make this happen?" And they did. It wasn't
easy… some sketchy moments…a lot of sacrifices. It was no cake walk,
but it was a faith walk. (And I'm not just playing with rhyme here.)

Now here I am, in the house. I can't believe it. And yet I'm having
one of those weekends that feels like that movie—"The Money Pit"—
a homeowner's nightmare. Flooded basement. And all my clothes fallen
off their rack to land in a big pile on the floor. I'm texting my
builder…he's on it.

"You're having a rough weekend. I'm going to send the guys in."

Obviously, I've got to get rid of more clothes. Maybe some of it is
baggage. I have more stuff in boxes in the garage. I'm wearing just a
few things, but…of course…I note, smiling to myself, with great
options to assemble different outfits and accessorize. The fashionista
spirit remains well-seated in this family. You know that by now. (We
have the photos to prove it.)

The repairmen are on the way.

And I walk through the house, praying.

CHAPTER THIRTY-THREE

MY BEAUTIFUL SISTER

Who had a hand in my building a house from the ground up? You might be surprised. At a critical moment in my life, everything hinged on kindly, timely conversations.

~

Family relations can get twisted into knots, hard to untangle. This is a sister story, about the ways Val and I, conversation by conversation, loosened the knots and formed new bonds wrapped in grace.

~

I built my house because my nieces offered me their family land. Not when I first asked about it, but later at just the *right* moment.

Remember the day when I was coming home from church, still holding the thought about God's timing from the sermon I'd heard? Remember my oldest daughter called me, and I was in despair. I'd lost the contract on the town house. She reassured me I would land well, somewhere in the middle of my family. (I had my doubts).

Well…as soon as she hung up, my sister called. (Remember?)

She still thought I was moving into the town house.

I picked up, "Yeah, I'm on my way home."

"When is the move, when are you moving into your house?" she asked. I heard the excitement in her voice.

"I'm not moving.

What do you *mean* you're not moving?" She started to cry. And then, these are her exact words: "Cernata, I don't know why all this is happening to you. But God is going to bless you, sis, he's got something bigger and better for you."

Her exact words.

In that conversation, my daughter had just got off the phone after telling me I was going to build a house from the ground up. And I'd just told her she was completely insane. Minutes later, talking to my sister, I couldn't stop crying. "I am just tired. The divorce mess. Everything piling up again. I just want to have my own home. I'm so tired. I feel like a failure."

Val said, "You're not a failure. You're not. You're a lot better off than I am." She says, "God is going to bless you, sister. I don't know how he's going to do it. But he's gonna bless you."

~

Many months later, there were two more conversations, one when my nieces offered me the land, and a second one that reveals my sister's loving hand.

On the day the family is sharing the news of the death of Mom Louise, I'm on the phone again with my sister and she asks if I had talked to Yvette, her oldest daughter, about the land her daughters had inherited from their father, and were about to lose.

And I say, hesitantly… "Yes…I talked to her way back…but it was the wrong time, she said they were going to do something else with it." My sister and I talk a little more about Mom Louise, and then she switches back to ask about the land.

"Yeah," she says, "they were talking about it again."

She's saying, "I heard my daughters talking…but I stay out of their personal business…and the only thing I said to them, "Have y'all thought about asking your aunt?""

And I say, "You said something to them?"

"Yeah. I just felt like, if anyone could do something with that land, it would be you, Cernata. That you were supposed to have it."

"Well what made you say that?"

"I don't know."

Apparently the two nieces asked their mom, "Do you think she'd want it?"

"All you can do is ask her," said my beautiful sister.

~

What I went through long ago with my sister led to this moment. This very moment. What we'd gone through was unjust. And in my small plane of understanding at the time, the unfairness to me was all I could see. Perhaps there is another story to be told about the rights of the young when their money is held in trust. Perhaps a story of justice with a different outcome. Someone in Virginia should have been held accountable for the disappearance of money put in trust for me. And someone should tell *that* story, because I don't want it to happen to another kid.

But God knew we were coming full circle, that I was going to meet someone to help me write this book and tell this whole story. When I was eighteen and discovered my college fund was gone, it seemed there were other plans for me: I would suffer. The hatred and the resentment would overwhelm me. Later on, in my new life as a young mother and wife, I was the one making mistakes. Well, God showed me, *You say you are one of my children…how can you say that you love me, whom you have not seen, when you cannot love my brother.*

Years after the loss, I knew I had to forgive my sister. And I had to tell myself, I had to *convince* myself, that God allowed what passed between us to happen to me for a reason. I don't understand it. For the life of me I don't know why it happened to an innocent kid. But God's timing is not our timing. After all, my sister is now in her 70s. But the same person *The Enemy* tried to use to destroy me, is the person whom God has used to elevate me. And it's taken all these years.

Truth is, I didn't feel it one hundred percent when I said, "I forgive you," for the first time. I was trying it out. And it was not a complete success; this was going to be a process, not an instant cure. But I knew I had to listen to God; I had to let it go. All of it. The anger, the pain. And the past.

When I spoke to her again, I told her how much damage she'd done to my life. And I told her that, despite it all, I forgave her. I believe if I hadn't, I would still be bound up with hatred and resentment.

I said to her, "I let it go...now you let it go."

There are days when I still see her beating herself up. In those moments, I try to persuade her to stop living in the past. "Let's just try to move forward," I'll say. "Stop talking to me about what happened, trying to justify what happened. I don't know why it happened. Let it go. There's nothing we can do to change it. Let it go."

~

She was the one who spoke to my nieces about their land. And who should have it...

My children know the story. My nieces know the story. But my sister was the one God used as a catalyst. She was the one who spoke to her children to say, "Have you considered your aunt?"

And look at the blessing that came from that.

~

But the first time I said something to her, mumbling something about forgiveness, the timing was wrong. I was just going through a lot in my marriage. There were some not so pleasant things happening. I didn't always make good judgments, and I was feeling regrets for things I had done. I was asking God to forgive me, because I could see that the discord between us was not in God's plan. Guilt settled in. I was holding on to resentment of what my sister had done to me. So, I said it—*I forgive you*—first in my twenties, when we talked over the phone. I meant it. Somewhat. Not whole-heartedly.

Twenty-five years later; my oldest daughter and I are talking. "Mom, I once heard you say to Aunt Val, 'I forgive you'. But I could also hear that anything that would remind you of what she did could make your anger flare up again. You could bring it slamming back to life, at the drop of a dime."

But my daughter was starting to see something new. "What I've noticed is, your temperament has calmed down. And the way you respond is calmer. "I've seen you grow."

"I'm just older. I've lost my edge."

But she keeps going, "Used to be, you were really smart and articulate, but your words would cut like a two-edged sword. Dad used to say that all the time about you. You were sharp and quick on your feet. And you could respond to anything and it would be just...*intelligent*.

"Hmmm," I say

She goes on, "You are cautious about telling the truth, careful about giving advice; your intent is not to hurt or harm."

She asks me—and this might have been ten years ago when we were living together—"Have you ever sat down and talked to your sister and told her how it made you feel, told her that you forgive her and that you want her to forgive herself?"

"Oh yeah, I've talked to her..."

"Ma, NOT over the phone! You have got to sit down and talk to her in person."

This is my middle child, who is very wise. And she thinks because she's the middle child, she must have suffered from that middle-child syndrome. Well, it's true, she has always admired her brother. He was super smart, athletic (and adored his little sister). But she's wise beyond belief. "You have got to sit down, Ma. And talk to her."

I took her advice.

~

One day I told my sister that I was going to spend the night at her house, because my job was right down the street. I gathered myself; I got myself ready to talk to her. And it was very uncomfortable. She broke down and cried all through it. I was crying but I had to get it out. I blurted, "I want you to forgive yourself. We can't live our last days like this. There's nothing I can do. I can't turn back the hands of time. I hated you at one time. I couldn't believe that I had a sister who could do that to me. But I can't allow this hate to cause me to go to hell. I just can't. Girl, it's not worth it!"

I told her, "I want you to stop bringing it up...and stop always saying, 'I was stupid, how could I have done that?'"

I keep going: "Sister, you're beating yourself up. And *that* is not God's way. That's *The Enemy's* way. He's trying to destroy you!"

She told me I was right. But from that day to this one she'll sometimes return to it, as if she can't resist its pull. "You know I didn't do everything right..." Hinting around. And I say to her, again, and as many times as it takes, "No one is perfect. God will forgive you."

~

You know, I often think about her. And I wonder. She lives in a seniors' building, located where we can all go see her. Her kids pick her up. She can still drive, so she does stuff. But she was the popular one. She had it all. She was vibrant and full of life. Now she lives alone, and by herself most of the time. Family is very important to her now.

She always jokes saying she is not what she was, and yes, her health is an issue. Arthritis runs really bad in our family. (I've had two hip replacements.) And she's had them too. Now she needs a knee replaced.

I say, "Hey, guess what? I'm getting this knee replaced."

She says, "I don't want them to cut anymore. I'm not doing that."

"But they're making the joints better," I insist, while she keeps waving me off.

"No more," she says, and she means it. We agree not to argue over the matter, while I go on about my attempts to sustain my health for the next few years.

~

Did she achieve her ultimate goal in life? It's hard to tell. It might be still ahead, still to come on her journey. But that ultimate conversation about forgiveness, was that all one conversation? Yes, after my daughter urged me to speak to her in person. But does my sister still think about it? I don't know. She doesn't bring up the old-time stuff as much anymore. After all, she spends a lot of the day by herself. We try to convince her to come out. I call her every day or every other day, during my drive time.

She was telling me the other day that she isn't feeling great anymore.

I ask if she's told the girls.

"No, I don't want to bother them," saying she can barely walk.

I say, with emphasis, "That's because of your *knee. You've got to get your knee fixed."*

We talk, just like sisters.

~

I once had a dream to go to college. And it was lost, so far gone from my heart and mind that I couldn't even spell the word.

Dream.

Remember? But here I am, and a new dream has become reality with substantial help from my sister. I've built my house from the ground up.

She's standing at the front door for her first visit. I hug her.

She smiles and says, "Thank you, God for blessing my sister!"

Each time Val visits me here I feel it all over again. Her blessing. She's been to every event and family gathering I've held at the house and even spent the night twice, once on Christmas, when I got up and cooked breakfast for her before she went off to enjoy a day with her children.

Our sisterhood is restored!

CHAPTER THIRTY-FOUR

WHO IS THE ENEMY?

Today, I am able to see certain things more clearly. Perhaps it is the wisdom of age. I hope so, and I recommend the practice. What might happen if we did look back over the years and attempt to see things clearly, without all the filters that have slipped in along the way?

You've heard me mention "The Enemy." What do I mean by that? I would define "The Enemy" in my life as the "spirit" of the devil. But in my early years I didn't identify "the enemy" as a spirit of the devil. I would look at individuals as being the villains who wanted to do me harm. Say my sister, or my father. I remember when there were disagreements in my family and I would blame Daddy for not making wise decisions and causing us pain. I would become angry and resentful. But as my parents always said, "What goes on in our house stays in our house." We never talked about anything negative. But all that did was to build up anger within me. Seen a different way, it was also developing in me a sense of tolerance, even numbness, that led me to accept what was happening with a sense of helplessness. It certainly led to vulnerability.

But once I began to read the Bible and apply myself to learning with an open mind, I began to understand it was the spirit of the enemy using those I loved dearly to destroy my life. I had to learn a lesson: "Derailment is not defeat."

But it would take years—so many years—for me to learn that each derailment was destined to push me one step closer to the women I was meant to be.

CHAPTER THIRTY-FIVE

A FRESH LOOK
AT A LONG MARRIAGE

In the moment, one senses events in one way. Over time, it can change. I can see things now that seem contradictory, but nonetheless complete the circle and reveal a more complex, multi-faceted truth.

The moral we learn from the story of my marriage—and it's a source of sadness, perhaps for us all—is that, mixed in with the difficult times, were many good times. And how to make sense of that? That a Friday night at home playing board games with the kids, or another with movies and popcorn, could later turn to argument. How to accept it all as truth? Can we understand life as a mosaic—an incomprehensible mix of emotions and experiences that, seen as a whole, can become— even—beautiful?

Look at the pure love in our family gatherings, our family and friends joining us for Christmas Eve, the birthday parties, yearly summer vacations, numerous church events, visits to amusement parks and the many long, winding drives through Virginia's lovely hills toward Lynchburg to visit my then husband's extended family.

And the fond memories of the year we drove to New Hampshire to visit my cousin. Or, in another year, the family vacation on Martha's Vineyard. Ah, The Vineyard! We had a phenomenal time—exploring the island, enjoying the cuisine, allowing the kids to enjoy this unique island community. I remember how excited and happy everyone was to be together with family and dive into a weeklong vacation on that island. We went back one more time afterwards and then never again.

Yes, we would always try to have a great vacation for the kids each year. Their dad liked to drive and would get us together to explore new sights each year. I remember one of the things he wanted to do when he retired was to purchase an RV and do that retiree thing. In his plan, we would drive across the country visiting any and every city on our list. Now I do need to clarify: this was *his* dream; I'm someone who preferred to fly, and while I'm at it, why not travel the world?

As a single woman, I've been able to do just that, to fulfill my dream of flying across the world to visit numerous countries. I've learned to live my best life and not allow anyone to place limitations on my dreams and desires.

Point made, I hope. I find life to be a mosaic of contrasting tones and textures. Can we see them all as one piece?

CHAPTER THIRTY-SIX

A KID'S EYE VIEW

I'm also fortunate that my kids have been able to perceive their parents' long marriage, and their own childhoods, each through his or her unique lens. My youngest daughter, Zelexis, has been willing and wonderfully able to articulate her experience. I'm delighted to make room for her here, in a chapter she calls…

THE MORSE CREW

FAMILY TIME. I'll always and forever be happy that I am part of the Morse family. One memory I treasure is the time my entire family drove to New Hampshire to visit my Cousin Paul. What started as a normal family road trip ended up being, maybe, the longest road trip ever. Back then the world didn't have smart phones so…North we went. So far north I could have sworn we were close to Maine. My dad was lost. But it wasn't a problem, we just turned it into a photo op. Finally, we made it to my Cousin Paul's house where we spent good times making blueberry waffles and playing with horses while the guys were in the woods doing God knows what. We ended the trip spending a few days in Martha's Vineyard. I still have pictures from the trip ready to show the world when I want to go back down memory lane.

DAD. It's kind of hard to give one example of why my dad is the best dad ever! He's always been there since Day One. My dad was a mechanic who worked for the transit system, but he also helped people around the neighborhood with his mechanic's abilities by working on their cars in our backyard. He often took me to the parts store where he taught me about the different simple aspects of a car that I would need to know about when I got older. Even though my dad was working, I thought of the time we spent as just bonding time. We would go to 7-Eleven to get a Slurpee and then head to someone's house to work on a car. My siblings and I would stay in the car the majority of the time, but sometimes we would be able to get out and play.

When I got older, it was time to put me to work. Around the age of 13 or 14 my dad started giving me assignments to complete during the summer. One summer we painted a bus for a school and reupholstered the seats. The next summer we reupholstered a bedroom set for my room, which was the first bedroom set my dad ever bought. The summer projects were fun…we even started a lawn service together. All summer I would wake up at 5 am and go to work with my dad on Friday through Sunday.

Now it wasn't always work when it came to my dad. He played a lot too. When we were kids, he made sure The Morse Crew had the biggest and baddest water guns available! Yes, that's right, the water guns with the back pack! My cousins would have parties in the park and we would have water gun fights. My dad would always show up with the biggest water gun, winning the fight of course. And if my dad wins then that automatically means The Morse Crew wins too, because we are a part of him, right? Right!

My dad was king of the dad jokes. He would tell a story and everyone listening would be waiting to see what was going to happen at the end and then BOOM…. It ended with a joke! Not just any joke, but the corniest joke you would ever hear. I find myself with the same spirit now. I just want everyone to have fun and smile. If I have to crack a joke to lighten the mood, I won't hesitate.

These times with my father taught me to be independent yet humble and never to be afraid to get your hands dirty. I believe that the times spent with my father instilled in me a work ethic like no other. Work long and hard. And after that, play hard!

MOM. Oh, a mother's love. My mom is the mom that everyone else wants. The children in the neighborhood always loved her. She was always there, at PTA meetings, soccer games, and church. You name it, she was there. Now that I think of it, she was balancing a lot, especially after my grandfather passed. (My grandfather had been the one who would watch after my siblings and me the majority of the time when both of my parents were at work). But mom made the time always to be active in our lives, especially when it came to school. Both of my parents were big on school but my mom was the enforcer. She insisted on us doing our best in all things "school" and she expected nothing less.

At the end of my elementary school my mom lost her job at PBS and she decided to go back to school to finish her Bachelor's degree. I always knew she was a wonder woman, but in my eyes, this showed the world what superpowers she actually had. From my middle school through high school my mother worked on and then graduated with her Bachelor's and Master's at the top of her class – all while being a mother and a wife. She never skipped a beat. She was always right there at all of my basketball games, even when I wasn't that great, making sure I played and had everything I needed. She not only mothered me but she would mother others in the neighborhood as well. I remember when I was on a team with a girl who didn't have the best living arrangements at home. Her mother was never home and my mom ended up taking her to and from practices and games. There was a time when that friend stayed at our house for a while since her home wasn't the best environment. Even though we didn't have a lot, Mom managed to open our home up to someone who may have needed it more.

If you know my mother, you know that she is a boss. She demands attention when she walks in the room. I believe that I get my leadership skills from her. I was raised to "set yourself apart from others" and always to strive to be better today than you were yesterday. Even while excelling in life she has taught me to love and support others: never to stop serving your community and to have a giving heart. There have been many times when I've seen my mother give her last to help others and I will never forget that I was given this platform to be able to assist others in the time of need. My mother is a walking example of the fact that your past does not dictate your future. There is always light at the end of the tunnel as long as you're willing to work to get there. And when you get there, mom still sets the example: walk through it with style and grace.

WATCHING. From a child's perspective, I thought my parents were perfect. Both of them were always around; we never went without anything we wanted and needed. Life was pretty much good. As an adult, I now know there were times when we may not have had the most and I understand the reason why both of my parent worked two jobs.

My sister calls me "the joy" of the family. I didn't understand that until I went to college. I believe I was born into the Morse Family to bring just that, joy. As a child I would be the one who cracked a joke when sometimes we're heading down a wrong path in a discussion, just trying to bring light to the situation. I manage my feelings the same way now that I am older. Whether I wake up on the wrong side of the bed or not, I'll greet most with a smile and even a hug. Understanding that your burdens shouldn't be placed on anyone else is essential to living. "The show must go on"—that is a statement I live by. You can't change what happened in the past but you have control over your future. I constantly tell my family and friends that "I want peace when I come home." I believe that shows me taking control of my future, based on my past.

WE THREE. The Morse Crew—we are a unique group of kids. Each of us communicate differently, think differently, dress differently, but we love the same. We owe all of our success to God and both our parents. Our parents made sure we had the platform to excel in life, even if it meant they went without. They instilled in us core values and morals that we do not stray from. They groomed us to be adults who can speak freely, yet respectfully, who can demand attention—but stay humble. Our parents addressed each of us on the level where we are: my brother is more business/tech savvy, my sister is the creative genius, I am the witty, smart alec. They understood their children and allowed us to develop into successful adults, giving guidance along the way.

Our parents also taught us the value of family. No matter how far apart, we are always there for each other. During holidays, my sister is the sibling who keeps everything together since I am away at school. She does the grocery shopping and cooking with my mom. She makes sure that we spend adequate time with both parents. My brother always shows up, even when most of the time you think he won't make it, but for some reason he is always there. These days, I do a lot of the dictating (lol, the baby doing the dictating) just because I am away at school. I fly in and out often but it's always hard to leave my family.

One thing I love about my parents is the simple fact that they allow us to fail. They allow us to try to navigate the world, but they are always there with support. I always ask my mom "What am I going to do without you?" and she always replies, "You'll survive."

The crazy part is, she's right, because both of my parents taught The Morse Crew how to survive.

CHAPTER THIRTY-SEVEN

A PRAISE SONG FOR MY CHILDREN

IN PRAISE OF OUR SON, THE FIRST-BORN. Zack, has always been the wise soul, the protector of all the females in his life. When he arrived, he instantly stepped into the role of the child that everybody wanted. Remember, he was the first child born into the family in the twenty years since my nieces had grown up. They adored him. My dad was elated; it was almost as if this new baby boy was the "reincarnation" of his own son, lost so long ago. My father-in-law loved welcoming him as the first male Morse grandchild. This child was so energized, so full of joy. His Dad beemed. A lot was riding on little Zack.

We raised our family in the church, and they were all exposed to the power of public speaking. Sure enough, when Little Zack was around ten, he answered a call to get up in church to pray. I offered help, but he insisted on doing it alone. "No, mommy I can do it." They put a little step stool in place for him. That boy prayed heaven down.

Lately he's been thinking about going back to get his PhD and, given that he has a gift for public speaking, one can only imagine how such a passionate and profound speaker might use his gifts.

As a teen, he showed his gift for breaking down barriers between people. He just got along with everyone of all colors and persuasions; a very peaceful fellow and wise. From the very beginning of his life, an old soul. He made everyone feel as if he'd known them a long time. He went on to be popular in high school and a terrific athlete.

Academically, he shone: graduating with five scholarship offers, and finally choosing Clark Atlantic University.

Now, at 36, he's doing well in the IT universe where he is settled for the moment professionally. He may have graduate school in mind at some point, but he'll let me know in his own time. This first-born child has always made his own decisions, especially regarding academia. He's the father of two daughters, and he takes that role very seriously. In fact, he was recently honored with a Best Dad Ever award from Alexis Dobbins' KidsNeed2 initiative. The award's purpose is to encourage, honor and celebrate those dads who are advocates for positive co-parenting and who manage, even with busy lives, to give their kids 150%. While in Atlanta he worked with youth groups, and may come full circle if he takes up his plans to get a doctorate and begin teaching. He's a good guy and proud of me; he thinks that this is my time. And…he's fun to be with. Why because he'll always be my Little Zack!

IN PRAISE OF OUR MIDDLE CHILD, ZNADA. Of course she showed a touch of middle-child syndrome. The usual litany of doubts plagued her: Not good enough. Not as multi-talented as my brother, not as smart as my sister. But we moms of middle children see all of that as upside down and backward. This child is creative, intuitive, and practices the art of bringing people together with genius. Throughout her life she's been the Superglue of Love holding her families together, always checking in, always asking, "Is everybody all right?" She loves animals in a way that almost convinced me she should be a vet. This child could be Doctor Doolittle. Beyond that, she is completely at home in nature.

She was the athletic and lean member of the Morse crew. A high school track star. In her growing years, she didn't identify her beauty.

(Was it because of the glasses?) But by the time she got to high school, she was drop-dead gorgeous, and the boys noticed.

Znada is happily married now, with three wonderful sons. Her ability to see another's true self beyond the surface that disguises it, led us all into a walk by grace. In her teenage years, she fell in love with a guy I would not have chosen for her, but God had a plan. She saw the good in him, and ultimately when I broke through the ice of my attitude, a shift happened. Love prevailed. We welcomed him. He came to Thanksgiving and told us he'd never seen a family have such a gathering. Struggling with his home life, he could see a better path ahead and wanted to get on it. After Znada went off to college, he began to cling to me. He would help around the house in little ways, like extracting our new Christmas tree from its box and assembling it, just because he'd never done it before. They became pregnant when Znada was two years into college. Although this could have been seen as a disruption, the whole family gathered in support. I believe this child was meant to be in our family. Znada's big brother and little sister declared that God makes no mistakes. They promised us all it would be life-changing.

This young man desperately wanted to be the father he never had. A friend declared that I would be the one to lead this man to Christ. I had my doubts. But the friend insisted, "This baby is going to bless you."

In time, the young man decided he wanted to go to church. And he would call at all hours to say he would be there. This might be on Sunday morning, when I was preparing breakfast. It became a habit with him; he would just show up. We'd turn and see him standing in the balcony. When church was over, he'd be gone.

But the look on his face when he first saw his baby son touched us all. He wanted to change his life; he wanted to be there for the child's dedication. He called me to ask what should he wear for the occasion? He said, "I'll meet you there, at the church." Young Zack said, "You'll be sitting with us." As the service proceeded, something nudged me, *turn and look to your left.* Sure enough, he was coming down the aisle to give his life to Christ. But as much as he struggled to do right, he died tragically, a victim of his hard life.

Since then, I've seen my daughter grow up into a powerful woman. Under no circumstances will she allow anything to bring her down. When I was sick, unable to get out of the bed, I remember this tiny-framed woman helping me up and into the shower, where she proceeded to scrub me down.

Znada has put the pedal to the metal, becoming a phenomenal mother. And as life would have it, a previous college friend came back into her life. A soldier. Now they are married and raising three sons. Znada works hard to integrate everyone into the wholesome family she always wanted.

Since then Znada has launched her own beauty line, a dream come true. I'm overjoyed at her accomplishments and sacrifice to fulfil her dream. The best is yet to come for my BabySis.

IN PRAISE OF OUR YOUNGEST, ZELEXIS. This beautiful girl had to grow up after her parents' breakup. She chose to go to North Carolina A & T university in Greensboro, North Carolina as her sister headed overseas to join her husband. For a while "Little" Zack was back home after completing college seeking employment. But all the good intent their dad and I poured into them has served them well. After our breakup, my ex and I were both sick. We were two strong parents fighting for their lives. And the children? They had to survive.

Zelexis is observant, a little bossy, with a tad bit of tattling thrown in. But the two sisters are very close; they have the close sisters' relationship I always wanted with mine. They do it all together. Znada launched her own makeup line over a year ago, with Zelexis encouraging her to go on and do it. Risk it. And I've thrown some marketing know-how into the launch. Znada gleaned the business aspects from me, and the just-right dose of risk-taking from Zelexis.

I'm proud of Zelexis. She had to go through a lot of stuff by herself. And the brunt of the divorce hit her when she was just heading off to college. After she completed her Bachelor's, she stayed on to apprentice in a dental practice, and then got certified as a dental hygienist. She will be a full-fledged Doctor of Dentistry soon, with plans to be a maxillofacial surgeon, or something on that order. Her bedside manner is wonderful. Like her dad, she inherited that ability to make you smile. (Each one of these children has their own "let me entertain you" style. Zack is understated, while Znada is boisterous and loud. And Zelexis is like, "You think that's funny? Really?") They like to have fun.

Now my kids are talking about goals and dreams when they get together. They're asking, "How do we take all we've received and turn it into something good?"

These days when they deal with their parents, they don't take sides. They might even choose not to be involved in these dialogues between "exes." They want to preserve a good relationship with each of us. And I know they'd love to see the day when their parents---and both of their significant others---are in the same space, and all is well. Only then, will the nightmare of being a divorced family be over.

THE FEMALE BONDS. Znada had a chance to see her mom in a new way when we lived together for almost five years. And that's when Znada could see what I was like when I was finally free. "Something came over you, Momma, you've changed. It was like a weight was lifted off your shoulders." She saw me start putting the negative things in the past of my life aside. (Well, I had to, my health was on the line.) That bond between the two of us, forged in those years, will last a lifetime.

It took Zelexis a while to come home to that first apartment. Znada, on the other hand said, "Not until I grew up and became a mother and wife, did I get it. I realized what you went through as a mother." But Zelexis had to grow up first, be a young lady. To experience loving, and being disappointed. She had to learn, "I can't judge anyone." It was a process of growing. When asked for advice I always said, "I'm not your friend, I'm your mother. *I ain't ya girlfriend.*" They laugh about it.

Now Zelexis is my biggest champion; she wants me healthy. Zack says as long as his mother is well and happy, we're all fine. That's all they want.

It's taken time for all of us to heal.

I couldn't ask for better kids. As the old folks say, they come from good stock.

CHAPTER THIRTY-EIGHT

ARE YOU BENT OUT OF TRUE?

I welcome you as a companion on this journey—not yet complete—as I confront my life and the ways it was bent out of true, out of its intended shape, like a piece of fine wood in the hands of a bad carpenter. The culprit? Others' expectations. Like you, perhaps, I've spent my life trying to defy those expectations to shape the person I am meant to be.

A MEDITATION FOR TODAY

How do we discover the shape of the life we're meant to have? Do you remember the quote above taken from the forward to this book? It is at the center of everything written here. I hope it will prompt you to think about the expectations of others that might have bent you "out of true"—a carpenter's expression for woodwork that's gone awry. Simply said, you were meant to be one thing, but became another, nowhere near satisfying, or no longer satisfying.

Getting it right might have to do with stepping into your true purpose. It might mean leaving a lot behind. (All the boxes of stuff in your garage from that last move, metaphorically speaking.) Once I started moving toward education and its benefits, I shed the mindsets that no longer served me, inspired by my professors and fellow students. Now that I'm a professor, I keep adding to my skill sets as I work with talented students who are as confirmed in their purpose as I am in mine.

What would you see if you looked back to find the first hint of your own purpose? The "who" you were meant to be.

Perhaps it showed up early as mine did, but faded as life moved on. I first met my purpose in my elementary school, a structure one city block wide on four sides. It was big! But on one corner of that block a section was set aside for kids judged physically or mentally disabled. I would always wander across the blacktop and play with those little kids. And I would get in trouble for it.

But my heart couldn't be held back any more than my mother's could; she would reach out to anyone she felt needed an extra special touch. I guess I caught the knack, because I always had a heart for those whom society deemed not good enough, "less than" others, when they were simply less fortunate. I also felt as if kindness was required when dealing with people suffering from whatever.

In my personal story, alcohol, mental and physical abuse cannot go unmentioned.

It's said that we can't help others if we can't help ourselves. So, I've worked on that one. I'm saying simply: there was a time when I held a glimmer of hope that I could help people. Now I'm more certain of it. I want to prove society's doubts wrong. I want to prove that if you give someone a second chance, they will soar. Not everyone will take that second chance. But, for those who want a chance to have their gifts nurtured, developed and empowered most of them soar like none before. This theme has risen through my life: I will help; they will flourish.

WHY NOT BE YOU? BE DIFFERENT. AND SOAR!

Does this resonate with you? It does for me: it powers me forward. I have always connected with those who are somehow "different". Is that because I felt "different" growing up? On the other hand, we could say I was actually always who I was meant to be, but didn't know it. Was I just spending overtime in the not-so-lovely-duckling stage? Tall. Big. Awkward. Not like my sister, not the swan. But what my life proves is—by God's grace—I was given a chance to fly, and I soared. Opportunity popped up and I grabbed it. I believe that's what my life demonstrates: all I needed was the right leaders around me. Now my purpose is to be that for others.

Once again, I assure you, if you position yourself to fly, you will. Look back at the young Cernata you met early in this story. Once my mother closed her eyes, I went right through the floor. And my rock bottom lasted *way* too long. Oh … really? Wasn't God doing the timing? Of course. Once I got the opportunity to soar, I did. Yes, I tripped over the bumps. I fell, and got back up. When I needed inspiration, I would conjure up the faces of my kids. Reassured that I was walking the journey for them, my steps picked up some "fly".

My goal now is crystal clear. I am here to leave a legacy for my generation and the next. And…the one after that, as the good work passes from hand to hand. I want you, dear reader, never, *ever,* to allow anyone to keep you from your destiny. To bend you out of true. The dream is yours. It might be deferred, but it will not be destroyed.

People, you *got* to keep that light burning.

HOW DID THIS HAPPEN?   WAS I "FRAMED?!"

Now the detective in me steps up to help. And I suspect that something in my story will resemble yours.

I distinctly remember when I was in grad school studying the theories and theoretical frameworks of leadership. When you look at the founding fathers of this work, like Maslow and his theory of the "hierarchy of needs," you discover much about yourself. I did. I learned, in a flash of insight, that we humans act in certain ways based on our strongest need in a given moment. For example, that need might sit on the rock bottom: the need for survival—food, water and shelter. (That was me, on the street.) Or, further up the hierarchy, the need could be self-actualization, and, at a later stage, self-transcendence.

Many theorists talk about human behavior. When I dug into that, I realized we are creatures who are, by nature, products of our environment. We desire the same kind of outcome as the person whom we observe receiving rewards, say, for a certain kind of behavior or simple good looks. (Doesn't it seem, sometimes, as though an attractive person walks a smoother path through life?) We observe this, we absorb the lesson, and adjust our actions to get the reward. Everyone wants to be rewarded, just not always in the same way. Some go for the money, some for the emotional bliss. These are my examples. You can add your own.

Studying theories of human behavior, I was struck by a concept which I then gave a name: "framing." In my research and writing, I've continued to be fascinated by how we, as individuals, may be "framed." It's the process by which people get their needs fulfilled by meeting someone else's expectations of who they should be, and how they should act. Those expectations have power, whether articulated or not—often immense power.

After a life-time of reflection, I can see how subtle that framing of me was in my early years. I can see the admiration of my whole family for my beautiful, talented, sister. As a young girl, I knew I didn't have those attributes. And that insight changed my perception of myself. Is this resonating with you?

At the moment, during my post-graduate years, when the impact of that insight presented itself to me, it also presented an explanation for my lifelong discomfort with myself. I attributed that debilitating discomfort to having been framed. Using a different metaphor, the one I prefer now, I had been "bent out of true". Bent out of God's intended shape for me. I could finally see that my problems had always turned on my efforts to shape myself to the expectations of others. I might as well have been insisting on wearing a dress that didn't flatter my body.

(Thank goodness, as long as my mother was sewing my dresses, that didn't happen.)

But, just now, I am prepared to flip this on its head. What if I framed myself? Wow! What if we all frame ourselves by craving the attributes of someone we aren't? And, in doing that, what if we can't help but land in a big puddle of dissatisfaction and lifelong unease?

Once I wanted to be something I wasn't. Now I don't.

And with all my heart, dear reader, I hope this is true for you.

~

In my childhood, my parents didn't know what I was thinking. They must have been puzzled, when they had a moment to think about it. They were raising kids in a time when most believed that kids ought to be seen, but not heard. I remember a family dynamic that required the expression of feelings and communication be very limited.

As a communicator, I tend to portray more Gen X characteristics. Add to that the "edge" picked up as a defense mechanism during my time on the street. But just before my mother died, I had started to challenge her way of thinking about kids and what they needed to be doing. I would ask questions. I'd begun to come out of my shell, raise my hand and actually *ask questions*. And get in trouble.

In the midst of that tentative psychological growth spurt, my mother's death landed like an atomic bomb. I collapsed backward. Flattened. And went right back into my shell.

Here's another example of being framed. My first love had an earlier wife who was petite. I wasn't. In my mind, because I was big and she was tiny, I felt he must be ashamed of me. See how the situation framed me? Why else would I always choose to be around people who devalued me? Why else would I tolerate that? Was being framed a self-fulfilling prophesy?

~

Even at nineteen, when I first had an inkling that I could sing, that I could be on stage, that I was developing... a voice...why couldn't I see that here was a real possibility to use a God-given talent? Instead, I accepted others' limited perceptions of who I could be.

The years rolled by, my journey took its twists and turns, from one dead-end to another, until I decided enough was enough. One fine day, perfectly timed, I got a glimpse of the real Cernata.

It came at PBS, when I got a chance to be part of a creative team. Working with them, I first experienced the kind of work I discovered I loved doing: it invited me to step out of my shell. The way ahead cleared, years of fog simply dissipated.

I'd started as Executive Assistant to the CFO, but I knew there was something more to be grasped; I just couldn't get my mind around it. It was taking a while to stretch up to my full height. But, once I spent time on a different floor, with the folks in the creative area, I caught the vibe. Creative work brought out the "fly" in me. It was just as I had glimpsed it at Howard University, with an all-too-brief sojourn backstage. Something in that experience had tugged at me—powerfully. Now I felt it again, once I'd found my way to the creative area at PBS. I was in my element, relaxed, happy, ready to release my gifts. The moral of my story can be anyone's: be in your element. You'll know you're in the right place when it brings out your "fly".

MY "FLY" IS THE STUDY OF LEADERSHIP.

In my academic studies, especially during my PhD program, I discovered a passion for the exploration of leadership: its concepts, its applications, all the ways you can get it wrong, and the thrilling, business-changing, life-changing things that happen when you get it right.

I've worked in enough facets of leadership in real-life scenarios to think it's fair to call myself an expert. And, most recently, as a consultant in the field, new scenarios constantly pop up with fresh examples of leadership done well. In my various assignments, I've also experienced cases of dysfunctional leadership. My long, varied experience has convinced me that there has to be a better way to train the next generation of leaders. This new crop must understand how to tap into their own emotional intelligence. Experience has shown such individuals—armed with their own insights—to be the most effective. They know the profound importance of communicating clearly. They engender the best employees, setting examples with their own behavior. The good leader knows how to nurture, motivate and stimulate. Most importantly, they create an environment of growth for each member of their team, including their direct reports.

Ironically, all of the human behavioral elements needed to grow productive members of society and the work force are exactly those things that were taken from me at a very young age. Can you now appreciate, dear reader, why my journey to regain them has been so long, complex—and determined?

And can you now appreciate why yours might also be complex, and not easy to grasp? But that doesn't have to be the end of your story. Keep on walking; discoveries are waiting.

CHAPTER THIRTY-NINE

HOW I FOUND MY VOICE

Howard University was not my default school because I did have other choices, including some offers of scholarships to other schools. But there was tension in the air, because in '73 and '74, the schools had just been integrated. I selected Howard, and its School of Fine Arts. I was in the 101 classes and I joined a choir, in fact, two. Though my A-side was possessed of a big personality, I had a B-side best called "shy". And we know I didn't think of myself as beautiful, not with my sister hanging out in my side mirror.

I remember sitting in a music theory class as my professor, Dr. Norris, posed this question: "How many of you think you're going to be a star?" Of course, everyone raised their hands. He paused and drew out his response. "Maybe ... just maybe ... one of you will make it. The rest of you will probably wind up teaching." He pushed again, "Well, what do you want to be?" Various responses popped up from the class. "I wanna be an R & B singer." Etc.

But what happened when he let some reality in and shared the odds of being a star? The students who were not totally bought into standing under a spotlight, not *absolutely* committed to pursuing a career as a professional vocalist—and that was a whole lot of us—all changed our major!

I remember being in the Fine Arts building, preparing for a rehearsal in my gospel choir, putting music on the stand, and thinking about the three lives I was juggling. One, here I am in school getting ready to sing. Two, I'm at home, in a relationship with an undermining man who doesn't want me to be successful at school. Three, I'm working from 1 to 9 pm at the bank. Three lives! I would rush to Howard, park in front of the Administration building, go to class from 8am till noon, and then drive back from Washington, D. C. to Virginia to my job. And then go home to the not-so-positive environment in the apartment I shared with my boyfriend. When was there time to study? None. No time for studying, because this boyfriend was jealous of any time I didn't commit to him. And—he was pulling on me, pressuring me, to marry? (Thank heaven fate intervened with a punch to the jaw. Ow!)

In contrast, my life at the School of Fine Arts was a place where creativity ran free. Even though I'd changed my major to something "practical"—business—the world of theatre and music exerted its powerful pull. I know now that the stage is a place where you either catch a dose of inspiration and blossom, or wrench yourself out of its grip.

That's where I caught "production fever". I fell in love with the stage. I wanted to work on the crew, in wardrobe, helping actresses with their costumes. Other friends were into stage props. I'll admit it right here: I just wanted to goof around and play with all those drama and music students. It felt so good, so right, as if it were meant to be.

~

So, a couple of guys, fellow students, would grill me, "Cernata, why have you changed your major?"

"I don't wanna teach."

"But you got the presence."

Picture this: I'm wearing jeans and a Howard University sweater with a baseball cap pushed down over my long pony tail. I am Total Tomboy.

One of the guys says, "I wanna do something different with you. I'm sick of you with the baseball cap."

"What do you mean," I say, "I'm cool, right?"

He's like, "Nah." Real clipped, short

He has something on his mind. He turns me around, away from the mirror on the dressing room wall, and starts doing my makeup. Out goes the ponytail—one of my two default stylings, the other being a full 'fro. And when he turns me back to the mirror, all he says is… "Look at yourself."

I will never forget it.

"Look how beautiful you are."

I default to: "I'm o.k. But I'm such a big girl."

So, work…with…what… you've got." (He does lean on this point a bit.) "Stop with the *'I'm such a big girl'* stuff!"

I don't remember his name, but I remember his meaning.

He ends his homily, "You're one of the coolest people we know."

I guess I was just all over the place, pulled and torn, trying to hold down a job, trying be a so-called "wife," at the age of 19. No wonder I couldn't see the wisdom when he said, "You're selling yourself short."

I didn't see myself as an artist, or even as someone who had a voice. Any kind of voice. For various reasons, I just couldn't see it. My sense of self-worth was cloudy. I was a big city in smog. That's when I transferred out of The School of Fine Arts into "business".

~

Dr. Norris wanted me to pursue voice, he really did. I might have been one of the stars who didn't fall back on teaching. (Which is, of course, a noble profession, not to diminish it in any way. After all, I'm a professor now.) But my dad got sick; he had one heart attack after another. And in any case, I seemed intent on running from my destiny.

I remember a day: I'm walking across campus, wearing my uncomfortable contacts and a pair of sunglasses to cover my black eye.

(Quick bit of stage setting: there's a place at Howard right in the middle of The Yard, called, The Wall. It's between Crampton Auditorium and the Fine Arts Building, on a pathway everybody takes.)

One of two football players strolling by notices me. Or rather he notices *us*, because I'm with my girlfriend, Janice Little, who is about 4'11. I'm 5'11+. In silhouette, walking across the campus, Janice and I looked just like Mutt and Jeff.

So, one of the football players says, "Why you wearin' sunglasses and it's cloudy?" He snatches them off and sees my black eye. "What's goin' on with you!" he wants to know. Of course I've been trying to hide the fact that I am in this toxic relationship; I am embarrassed to admit such a thing. "Why, would you allow somebody to do that to you?" And I'm just, like, "Well..." making up excuses... "maybe I shouldn't have said what I said to my boyfriend."

And there you have it, dear reader, the classic picture of tolerating abuse.

~

A lot was going on with me then. I didn't do well in the school of business. I did try hard, but the timing was off. My dad seemed always to be sick or on the verge of it. Bottom line: my inner voice—and the voice I spoke with—had both gone silent. There was too much standing between me and anything called insight. I simply had no way of discovering who I was.

On to the next chapter.

I became a wife and a mother who said prayers for her children and herself, prayers that she'd be capable of raising these kids to become vibrant and productive. That they might even be citizens who soar.

Once I relocated my misplaced voice, once I broke away from old habits and from people who meant me no good, a momentous shift gradually happened. Education had a lot to do with it. I morphed into a different person. Having grown up in the church with the abiding faith it engendered, my paradigm shifted once I was exposed to academia. Dr. McCollum had assured me: with success comes sacrifice. "You're going to change. You'll be a critical thinker, meaning you'll process information more in-depth. Your circle will change."

Now, listening to podcasts focused on a host of success stories, I see that, yes, one's family and friends can—sometimes must—change. However … in the African-American community there's a "particular" dynamic in play. When there's been a certain "shift" and you're perceived to have "stepped away", no longer "running in the same circles", perhaps when you've elevated yourself to a different economic or educational level, you're labeled "bourgeois". And, slowly, that began to happen. Education exposed me to different—soaring—opportunities—and stresses.

Take this example: My daughters and I have vowed every year to go to a different place. They say, "Mom you work hard, you're always giving, taking care of everyone else, you need a vacation." But when we do that, some, who may be watching us, have been known to form a "certain perception" that's not always one of unbridled admiration.

Perceptions can be tricky to sort out. In our lives, there's been what we had, what we hoped to have, and what we worked to have. According to what society saw in my younger years in The Berg, my family had a Wurlitzer piano, my dad had a new car every four years, and we were all well-dressed. But we lived in the projects. From TV, I knew there was yet another life, not just cozy and comfortable and community-centered, but one with big houses, big cars, etc. Inevitably, we equated all that with the European race. Yet, back in The Berg, though our home may have been small, it was scrupulously clean, giving us precious reason to be proud.

But we're talking about how I found my voice, and how you might find yours. OK. Maybe there are options right in front of you, hiding in plain sight.

Example: I got another taste of what that voice could do when I worked at the high school, after PBS. My supervisor, Dr. Johnson, gave me a platform, a place where I could build bridges and impact change. Remember, I had the skill of public speaking nurtured during my young years at church. It came fully into its own during an interesting incident.

No one who was African-American had ever run the high school graduation party, but I was going to do it that year. Some of the parents were concerned, but one of them had heard me speak, so she invited me to come and chat with a bunch of other parents.

It was a beautiful house, the family was wealthy, and our hostess was sweet as could be. When we went in and surveyed the long tables of food and drink, I was a bit uneasy. Dr. Johnson had come along and he said, "Just stick to your script and you'll be fine." But I was annoyed at the situation and the hostess to begin with, because … *why? Why* did she feel the need to hold such a party to explain *me* to these folks? *How dare you*, I thought, *I have a stake in this. My kids go to this school; my son is a star athlete. And don't forget the time I brought PBS to the high school during a NASA event.*

But I stuck to my script—with a few modest additions. Net, net: as the evening proceeded, all those people were grinning from ear-to-ear. The day after, the hostess called and asked me to meet for coffee. When we met, I sipped hot chocolate while she apologized, revealing that she had ripped them a good one— "them" being her guests—after the party was over and we'd left. "How dare we doubt her?" she'd said to them. "Ms. Morse is totally invested in this school!"

And she was right. Before I'd come on board as staff, I'd been working at the high school as a volunteer, and that parent knew I'd networked to get sponsors for all sorts of projects, including the all-night graduation party, which some kids could not afford to attend. Never before that year—2001—had so many kids been able to go. I'd checked in with kids who weren't on my attendance list. They'd told me, *"we can't afford it, it's just not for us."* I rolled up my sleeves and made sure every kid had the chance to go to that party—and feel comfortable. I even had some of our Muslim kids there. And we got a caterer to make sure they had their own food.

I did it for my son, my two daughters, and every kid who needed a hand up. (Can you see yourself here?)

All my efforts had helped me believe I had a voice to tell many an untold story. No longer just a notion, my presence in the school was making a difference for a lot of kids. But once I was back in school getting my Bachelor's and saw that PhD student go up on stage, it blew out all my stops; I recognized that the woman getting hooded as a new Doctor of Philosophy could be me. Of course, that would mean a different lifestyle, complete with many challenges, but it would be a lifestyle that fit.

Ironically, if I had not been laid off from PBS, I would never have launched myself on the road to higher education. In the high school job, I started at $17 an hour. But no matter, I was feeling the wind beneath my wings, becoming the voice for kids who did not have a voice. They were too busy to exercise their own voices, since it took all they had just to survive, with no money and no food at home. They were lethargic in class; they came to school because they were hungry and needed to be near a cafeteria. When I became the voice of the school, it was for those students.

It got to the point where students would sit in the hallway outside my office, waiting for me to show up. They wanted to talk, and specifically, to me. (That situation was not popular with their assigned guidance counselors, because the students were in the process of filling out their college applications.) While their counselors did work well with them, I could offer a special kind of encouragement given my own situation as a person who'd given up on college, with regret. I was pleased to support the other staff, including the tutors engaged to mentor the young athletes. Those young men and women were trying to change their students' lives. And soon enough that would be me. It was on a night when I was helping some kids fill out their applications that Dr. Johnson came in and spurred me to get going and complete my first college degree.

The next big shift happened once I got my Master's and was able to double my salary. I couldn't help feeling the positive economic impact. When I left my job at the high school, I went right into an ad agency. I then left that agency when I was recruited into the government by one of my clients. By then, I had my freedom: I no longer had to depend on another human being for economic support, an experience which, often, had been humiliating.

Most importantly, I had found my voice. You will find yours, if you haven't already. And when you have a voice, you're meant to use it. I urge my listeners to find their true selves, to shape the lives they are meant to lead. To follow a purpose. To speak out, for example, on a subject that moves you. In my case, that of domestic violence.

CHAPTER FORTY

LETTER TO A BEST FRIEND

Scene: Anytown, USA

Interior. A Family Home. Evening

Let us imagine…It could be happening now… *The dishes are cleared off the table. The kids are doing homework in another room. Mom is stacking the dishes in the washer. Dad comes into the kitchen and thrusts a stack of household bills in her face, then lets them scatter all over the floor. Mom, annoyed, raises her voice. He stuffs his face in hers. And the argument escalates into violence.*

The scene above isn't hard to imagine, especially since it doesn't just play out in the imagination. It's real, it's here, and it shows no sign of stopping. I have said that when you find your voice, it's important to use it to impact change. And that's why I'm here to speak up about domestic violence. Throughout this story, dear reader, I have thought of you as my friend. And that's why I'm writing my thoughts on this subject in the form of a letter to a best friend. Let's call her…

Etta:

You've been my friend for a long time, and I know you're in an abusive relationship because I see the signs. I can't keep quiet anymore. We have got to talk about what this situation is doing to you. You're a strong woman, so I'm asking you…why would a strong woman stay in this relationship? I've given this a lot of thought, so let me guess. For one thing, it would be just like you to take on the blame. In fact, I remember you saying, "Maybe if I hadn't said what I said, we wouldn't have landed in an argument. And he wouldn't have gotten rough with me." Really? Girlfriend, let me turn that around. Why does he think it's o.k. to react with violence to some statement he doesn't agree with? It worries me that he thinks he's going to shape-shift you into someone else, someone who will let him control you.

Or maybe he doesn't realize he is harming you, that he's destroying your self-worth. (I see that too.) You mean the world to me, Etta, but let me tell you, what you're experiencing now is just the start…it can—and almost certainly will—get worse. Right now, you feel like you're o.k., you're surviving. But there are very few survivors of intense, recurring abuse. And let me guess, every policeman in the area knows your address. And they're surprised because everything about you says you shouldn't be calling 911, because you've got a nice house and all that. But, have any of them told you this has to stop, that they don't want to take you away in a body bag?

Think about this: you have to protect yourself. Because no one else can. You've said he is very controlling. I'm saying, you have got to get away from him. Even if you're not ready to call him "an abuser," he needs help. What if there is some mental instability that needs to be treated? Are you the one to do that? You're not a mental health professional. Does it feel like he has an unhealthy obsession with you? Whatever, you can't make the diagnosis. I've heard you say he's the perfect father. And you can't leave the kids. I get it. But, long term? Short-term? You think it's getting better, maybe you think everything will work out "somehow". But caution: do you even understand everything that is going on? I know you still love him because you've told me so.

But…are there red flags, something he told you earlier? Seriously, Etta, when a red flag shows up, or your intuition kicks in, pay attention, this could be a matter of life or death. Because, guess what? Not everyone who's abused gets to walk away to tell the story. If you don't do something now, when you can, you're doing yourself a disservice as well as everybody around you. And the person who's perpetuating this behavior? They need help! Nine times out of ten, they are good people. They're just being controlled by---who knows what? A chemical imbalance or hey... The Enemy? Some demonic spirit? Who can know? Maybe they need counseling, or medical help. But you *can't counsel them because you are the one being victimized. I have to ask: are drugs or alcohol involved? If so, they need help. Addiction to substances is very often a big piece of abuse. You can't fix that piece for them.*

So, I've been told: "when you see it, say something; when you see it, do something." That's why I'm writing to you. I want you to protect yourself and those you love.

Think of the stories you've read about people whose habitual acts of violence were condoned and accepted, only to pile tragedy on tragedy by killing themselves as well as the people they loved. It's a sickness; your abuser needs help. But you can't help the person whose hurting you if you're so heavily involved with him. The worst outcome of your situation would be that you see the signs but convince yourself nothing really bad will happen...until it does. What you see is what you get, Etta. And that's what all of us need to understand. I would say this to anyone who's in a situation like yours: if you're seeing signs or experiencing direct acts of violence, no matter how 'small,' you'd better take it very seriously.

Respectfully, Your friend, Cernata

Violence of any kind is horrible. (You know I speak from experience.) Both mental and physical violence will have a life-long impact on all involved.

And, please do not forget: Domestic violence can be deadly. No one should risk their lives, not a man or a woman, to stay in a violent relationship. But, no matter the circumstance or how you may rationalize it, the truth is: no one has the right to lay hands on another human being with violent intent.

I do not believe a person who has experienced domestic violence will ever forget when, where, and how the act was committed.

And I've learned this: Any healing comes with the ability to move forward in life and regain a sense of what is normal. I have found, that when you're trying to build a new relationship, you must be mindful of the "leftovers," the remnants of the experience that can poison your effort to shed the past and build something new. Still, be aware; keep trying. It's your one life. It's worth it.

CHAPTER FORTY-ONE

THE FINAL ACT OF LOVE
IS FORGIVENESS

One Sunday, I hear a sermon on love and forgiveness. And so of course I immediately start thinking about my life, my journey, and pose the question: can I forgive myself? For years a gloom of unforgiveness had hung around me, starting from the time I lost my mom. I was angry, blaming God for taking her. As I began to grow into my teenage years and make unwise decisions, my anger turned on myself: I began to beat myself up. It had always been so. My mom always said, "You never have to worry about Cernata, she'll tell on herself." One story illustrates that very well.

I'm back in The Berg, 11 or 12 years old, participating in the rite of passage called, "learning to smoke." We're all outside, and I'm not sure about the plan. "Girl, just take a puff," someone says, and I inhale deeply. Once. Maybe twice. Then the streetlights come on and my mother's voice rings out on cue. I try to bolt, but she sees me. I dodge and weave, mostly heading home, but not directly. She calls again; I change course again, with a new plan to head right up the stairs and into the bathroom to brush my teeth. That done, I'm still in there flapping my clothes, desperately trying to free them of the smell of smoke, when my sister's banging on the door means surrender. It's over. My cover is blown. So, we go sit down at the table. I reek of smoke. My sister complains to my mom, "I know you can smell this smoke." My mother reminds her to be patient, that Cernata will eventually confess. And sure enough later that night, I burst out crying, "Mom, I got something to tell you!".

That little girl has always been with me. And it seems to have been part of my children as well, who each in their own style, are always eager to tell the truth.

But after my mom was gone, I was plagued by the notion that if you're a sinner, you're going to hell. It was the old tradition that saw God as vengeful, dedicated to punishing sins. I internalized that unforgiving message for years, until I discovered God was loving, and quite willing to cast you in a sea of forgiveness.

Still, when I was first faced with the need to forgive my sister, I hesitated. The voice said, "Say it. Speak it." I complied but not with real intention. Instead I "tried it on." I spoke it, but I hedged. Sound familiar? The outcome was smudged. Not one way or the other. And here's an interesting thing to ponder: my sister might have been ready to forgive me for my mistreatment of her that had lasted for years. For the pain she experienced when my sharp tongue cut her down. She might have calculated, *Cernata didn't forgive me, so I won't forgive her.* Who would blame her for carrying her own bitterness?

And that's the point: If we don't forgive, we will carry bitterness. And it will eat us alive. It's that destructive, affecting every move we make as it works its way through us. It stymies emotional growth. Love shrivels; anger spills out. Instead, why not consider the manifold benefits of forgiveness? In a true and lasting act of love?

I did forgive my sister, finally, with a full heart. The scar tissue loosened its grip and allowed healing to begin. The sisterly bond could repair itself. Now, our conversations are sweeter. This year, again, she will share Thanksgiving with our family. She's already asked for her favorite treat made by *me*, the legacy baker schooled by my grandmother and Mom Louise. (We're talking about my red velvet cake, people.)

And one more thing: she's found this new little church. I rejoice for her, though I'm puzzled.

"Why did you change churches?"

"Because I want to go to a place where I can use my talents and help the church grow. I think that's where I'm gonna be until it's my time to go."

"Why this little church?"

"I think God can use me there. It's small. Lots of elderly folks attend. I feel more comfortable there."

She's asked me to attend on the Sunday when the congregation extends the right hand of fellowship to receive her into the church. I'm going to be there. Our bond has grown stronger, though her guilt can still bedevil her.

"Let it go. Let it go. If I can, you can," comes my usual refrain.

"But you could have done so much more."

"Yes, but if I'd gone to California, I wouldn't have had my three wonderful kids. I might not be "Doctor C." I said it was hard, and I suffered, but God has blessed me beyond my imagination, just as Daddy and my godmother promised.

The only thing my dad wanted to see before he passed was for us to mend the brokenness between us. I believe we have. All it took was forgiveness, that final act of love.

~

Now that my husband and I are divorced, we are occasionally put to the test when we have to go to special family events together. Anticipating this, our kids are often stressed, because…what might happen if The Ex and I, a.k.a., Mom and Dad, are in the same place? It's still not predictable—sometime o.k., sometimes funny, sometimes weird—but so far, survivable. To be otherwise, we will have to let the old stuff go. All of it. And *that's* a lot of stuff.

There's a big test coming up, when my daughter graduates from dental school, and becomes Dr. Zelexis C. Morse. Wouldn't it be great if she could experience a moment of reconciliation as both her natural parents participate in the "hooding" ceremony? What if both sets of hands adjusted the hood on her lovely head? Wouldn't it be great if the three of us—and all those standing by to congratulate her—feel only the pride. No complications; only rejoicing.

We're working on it.

~

It's taken me a long time to learn that it's not about who did what to me, or why they did it, or who is "guilty" of transgression. It's about forgiveness.

When I heard that sermon about God's love and forgiveness, I pondered the fact that many Christians are condescending. They judge others, neither loving nor forgiving. And yet, I recall a very different response from the church in Charleston where a young man shot worshipers while they were praying, an act that defies understanding. But I saw this on the news: some of the parishioners' family came forward to speak up and say, "We forgive him. Because you can't love a dying world if we don't forgive them."

Then it happens again: human beings are shot in more houses of worship, in the First Baptist Church in Sutherland Springs, Texas, and in the Tree of Life Synagogue in Pittsburg. Some days after the shooting there, I'm getting ready for work, listening to the news, when two sisters of one of the deceased in Pittsburgh, come on the air. They pay tribute to their brother, a loving man who gave his all, not just in death but in life. He loved his community, loved his synagogue; he was always ready to help somebody. The sisters ask why this happened to him and the others. But one of them offers this astounding idea: we have to forgive the man who did this, because if we don't, evil prevails. "We don't want evil to win, we're going to have the final word. We're not going to let this hatred continue."

~

I want to end this chapter on a hopeful note. I want to offer my dear readers something to ponder. It's hard when you hear about some maniac who just wanted to kill somebody because their skin is a different color or they practice a different religion. But think about it. Shouldn't we have the last word? Evil cannot prevail.

The final act of love must be forgiveness.

CHAPTER FORTY-TWO

BEYOND THE FOUR BLOCKS

Seen in wide-shot, the first decade of my life, the 60s, was a time of tumult. The adults in my family could look beyond the four blocks of our neighborhood and witness events that would shape all our lives from that point forward. The Civil Rights Act of 1960, signed by President Eisenhower, strengthened provisions from earlier bills to protect our voting rights. In that same year, JFK was elected by a razor-thin margin. The Space Program was launched by the Russians in 1961 and, in 1962, we Americans survived the Cuban Missile Crisis. (And isn't it interesting to notice that those two countries are still embroiled in our history to this day?)

In the summer of 1963, Reverend Martin Luther King, Jr. advocated for our social and economic rights when he led the March on Washington for Jobs and Freedom…to the very foot of the Lincoln Memorial, seven miles from our home in Alexandria. Afterwards, when the country fell into chaos, we watched the coverage of protests, police actions, water hoses, and attack dogs. Through the civil rights movement, Birmingham, Selma, Detroit and L.A. burst into our living room on the little black and white TV. Later in 1963, JFK was assassinated. Johnson signed more civil rights legislation in 1964 and 1968. And in 1968, both RFK and Martin Luther King were assassinated, the country tumbling further into riot. By 1969, we had reached the moon.

That was the first decade of my life.

Seen in close-up, I was born into an era of segregation, but that fact did not define me. Why? Because my life was sheltered within the close community formed by our four-square blocks of The Berg and our small, crowded but comforting row house. As the wider world pressed in, my years of the 60s were tempered by luck. I was born into a very strong, loving Southern Baptist environment. I was aware that some people appeared to have more than we did, but I was comfortable. I began as a happy kid.

Still, I was not so sheltered that I was unaware of other cultures. Venturing beyond the four blocks, my life began to intertwine with others. My home built my foundation, but curiosity—what's around the next corner?—built the rest of my life.

Riding high on that little pink bicycle, I made my first moves beyond the "known world" when I visited Mr. Marty's, the Jewish family who lived over their grocery store. It was their kindness that I remember. When we were face-to-face with one another, we were color blind. I can't remember a conversation that might have indicated they were a Jewish family, or that we were somehow different from each other. All I knew was that they were "the Martys". Our interactions with one another were pure. Nothing resonated with me except: they were a family. They were part of my community and they did a lot to make it a neighborhood.

Of course, chaos poured over us with the death of Martin Luther King, Jr. and the riots that followed, stirring up hatred and divisiveness. But my mom, my grandmother and my dad, kept us anchored. They spared us most of the raw anger of the day's news, though some couldn't help leaking through. I wasn't plugged into the TV—and other media—quite in the way later generations are; my family kept us insulated from most of the media damage. Or, let's say, they put it into context, emphasizing the importance of voting and being an engaged citizen, of keeping up my health records, and so on. Through it all, the central idea that kept me rooted was, "always respect people for who they are." Do you remember the little moment with my grandmother, when she's rubbing her arm and saying, "Never judge a person by the color of their skin…" And then goes on to touch her hand to her heart, saying, "…but by the content of their heart." Remember? It's been with me and will be with me until it's my time to go. Sometimes it gets a little rough because people can be mean, you know, and they may judge you based on how you look and your size, and what they may consider beautiful. I suffered from that, but like preventive medicine, the seeds of love and forgiveness were planted in my life subtly, and at a young age.

Then, when the schools were integrated, I encountered other cultures within my classroom. I remember Rosemary, the vibrant young woman who was from a Jewish family; her father was an Ob-Gyn. She was just full of life and love. Since I always gravitated away from the norm, when someone might say, "Don't talk to her," I would do the opposite. And then there was Alexandra, very petite, whom I probably overpowered with my size. But I was drawn to her because she was different with her oversized glasses and her Beatle-cut hair. She was English and I loved her accent! And because I was kind, one day she told her mom and dad about me and invited me to her house. But guess *what?*…she lived beyond the four blocks. Within eyesight of Mr. Marty's. (He was on the corner of Queen and Royal, while Alexandra lived in one of the townhouses in Old Town between Royal and Pitt Street.) So, at that time I was interacting with a Jewish family and an English family from London. I don't know what's become of Alexandra but I hope the memory of her friendship with me, her first African American friend, has lasted her a lifetime. We shared with each other. She always wanted me to try the tea "biscuits" her mom would make, and of course they drank a lot of tea. And, being a Southern girl, I'd ask my mom to do her homemade rolls and jam for them. Her dad would bring me home on those evenings when we'd been studying late together. I actually could have walked home, but he wanted to meet my family. Once he did, he never turned his nose down on us. Maybe it was because of his military career that led him to different places around the world and opened his mind. Similarly, it was Alexandra's descriptions of her travels that stirred the idea within me to travel far beyond the four blocks. She showed me pictures of London and Paris, asking me if I'd traveled enough, telling me about that other world —over there—where "they would like you." She said they ate a lot of potatoes and roast beef. I'm thinking, *how am I going to get across all that water to get to that beautiful place?* And then I found myself thinking, *but they eat the same things we do.*

I think those interactions with Alexandra and Rosemary and The Martys set the stage for me to be open and to understand that the world was big and broad and beautiful and that there were people just like me—maybe from a different culture, wearing a different skin color— but essentially just like me. And what gladdens my heart is that I can see my next generation, my kids, who have just taken off, *exponentially,* beyond those four blocks. For example, my youngest plans to visit every single continent in the world before she lays down her maps. And she wants to get the three of us women in the Morse crew to start the habit of traveling once a year to somewhere amazing. Just to chill. My son has traveled to Dubai and the Mediterranean through his work in cyberspace. And my oldest daughter and son have lived in Japan. My parents must be relishing all this in heaven: how far their family has traveled beyond the four blocks.

~

My eyes were truly opened by a trip to the Holocaust Museum in Washington we organized for the school kids. Later, in one of my professional jobs, I was tasked with creating events for members of the organization. In that case, I was assigned the job of creating a Holocaust tribute. Knowing that history, I couldn't help connecting it to the history of enslavement in our country, thinking: *it doesn't matter the color of your skin, when you're ripped apart from your family and enslaved in*

camps; when your women are raped, and your men are tortured, when
you are demoralized and degraded, all of it is inhuman.

That notion connected with me profoundly. I had all the motivation
I needed to make that presentation special. Working with the director
of the museum, I located a Holocaust survivor, Mr. Marty Weissmann.
My initial interview with him gave me chills. So, bucking the usual
procedures, I went to my supervisor and suggested I make use of my
broadcast background. With the help of engineers, we recruited from
the organization, I proposed a short-form documentary using Mr.
Weissmann's visuals combined with an original sound track. I would
write a script based on the interview, and we would have Mr. Weissman
and others "voice" the track to build the story. My supervisors gave me
permission to go forward with my concept…if I could pull it off. I knew
myself well enough; my experience and determination would carry me
through. (I don't give up easily, but I've also learned that if I need to
give up, I can do that too.) You don't always have to push through. You
need to learn, as I say, "to stand still and let God take over."

I spoke to Mr. Weissman's wife explaining what we planned to do.
She started to weep. "He'll be so pleased."

I had produced a lot of promotion for the event. When the day came,
I was pleased to see the hall fill up to standing room only.

THE TAPE ROLLS:

I'm narrating the story, along with three other staff who volunteered to
be additional characters in the story. One of them recreates the voice of
Mr. Weissman as a little boy standing next to railroad tracks at the
entrance to one of the Nazi camps. The families are being separated into
two lines, men and boys on one side, women and girls on the other.
Marty moves to join his mother and sister, when a large German soldier
smacks him back. In short, the males in his family survived, the females
didn't. Mr. Weissmann has always believed the German soldier must
have had a snippet of humanity, because he struck Marty with a stick,
indicating he should stay put in his queue.

All Mr. Weissman can remember decades later were the boots and the stick. He assumed the soldier's act saved his life.

~

As the tape ended, everyone in that room was affected; not a dry eye anywhere. And Mr. Weissman, trembling, turned to me and said, "You listened, you heard me. And you cared."

I'd only met him a few weeks earlier. By the time the show ended, he'd become a hero to me and many, but he remained humble...even grateful...to the African American woman who listened closely in order to tell his story well.

I see a direct line from Mr. Marty at his grocery store, who introduced me to the Jewish culture, to Mr. Marty Weissman forty years later who would collaborate with me to bear witness to his own story of life and death, seen through the wide-open eyes of a child. I didn't fear him because he was different, because he was Jewish. That didn't occur to me. He was a man who had a story, and I was allowed the chance to help tell it.

The experience transformed me, starting from the moment when I stepped through the doors of the Holocaust Museum, and began to see, in striking relief, the connection between their WWII history and our centuries of African-American enslavement.

Some might disagree—there will always be disagreement—but I felt the connection. And I wanted Marty Weissman to know that. To contemplate these two all-too-similar stories was gut-wrenching to me. The stories of enslavement have been passed down along the generations, to many who are no longer living. But here was Mr. Weissman in front of me. Alive. And I could hear his story, hug him, and thank him.

I drove him home. As he was getting out of the car, carefully, to spare his elderly joints, we spoke briefly.

"I will never forget you, Cernata Morse."

"And I will never forget you, Mr. Marty Weissman."

Just as that journey runs in a direct line from an early Mr. Marty to a later Mr. Marty, so does the journey prompted by Alexandra. As a grownup, I did go to England. I saw the stained-glass, I saw the very first English Bible. Along with many a castle and Buckingham Palace, complete with the full Changing of the Guard. I visited St. Paul's Cathedral, among England's most magnificent churches, noting its beautiful architecture, a breathtaking arrangement of stone and glass. And...would you believe...it reminded me of the little churches down in Blenheim, Virginia, outside Charlottesville; like my great-grandfather's church Middle Oak Baptist Church. How can it be, I thought, that I'm three thousand miles away, but feel like I'm standing in the church of my great-grandparents?

Reverend Jones, I have journeyed far, only to find home again.

~

Ah, Paris. Our group is in a restaurant. The gentleman who works there sees me, asks me where I'm from and says, "I want to show you something." He disappears back in the kitchen. He brings out his mother, a very tall, very stout woman, elderly, with beautiful long gray hair. The shape of her face is identical to mine. I look at her and feel as though I'm gazing at my grandmother, or possibly at my mother, the way she might have looked had she aged. And the lady is looking at me and then just steps up and hugs me. "Have you ever been here before?" she asks. I say, "No, ma'am. This is my first time ever in Paris."

They wanted to take a picture of all of us together, because no one would believe this African-American woman who has never before been to Paris could so strongly resemble their family.

That was a trip filled with food to die for, welcoming cultures and reassuring experiences wherever we and our group of kids stopped for a meal, be it in France, Italy, or England. And, sure enough, in one of England's pubs, wonderful potatoes and pot roast showed up. (Just as

Alexandra had predicted.). On that occasion too, the proprietor looked at me and asked, "Have you been in here before?" My colleagues were amused, asking if I'd secretly snuck across the Atlantic to scout those countries earlier. I insisted I hadn't but, who knows, maybe I had. By spirit. Or imagination. Maybe my mind had wandered when I was with the first Mr. Marty and Alexandra and Rosemary. However, it all came to pass, things that I'd seen only in pictures were showing up in real time. All those photos coming to life for me.

~

So, let's look at this little girl who lived within the four blocks, not getting caught up in stereotypes. Let's see her forty years later, in England and Europe, far *beyond* the four blocks, walking in the shoes of history. There I was, sitting where Napoleon sat when he was carried to church on his throne. And standing on the balcony where he looked out on his peasants. Just amazing. (And somewhat amusing.) Reading history is one thing; walking through it, touching and feeling, is quite another. We stayed in Paris within eyesight of the Eiffel Tower, another postcard from my past come to life.

My advice…and remember I've weathered many a storm and many a winding road finally to arrive at wisdom…no matter what part of the country you're from, do yourself a favor…explore the world.

And don't allow society to put barriers around your mind. Resist the urge to get caught up in divisiveness. Love will conquer hate. I learned that from my own circumstances, growing up in segregation and forced integration. I experienced what young people experienced in Selma. (You didn't have to go to Selma to get that.) I was in Alexandria, Virginia in the 70s, in high schools where African-Americans were not welcome. That's the kind of life-changing time that marks you, when you begin to realize: I'm not welcome. There were no dogs. That was a Selma thing we didn't experience. But it takes time to shed the stress of the conflicted feelings: "I've got to get my education... but I'm not *welcome* here ... in the place where it has to happen."

I have survived because the seeds of understanding, planted long ago in The Berg, have flowered and carried me through life. I might have turned out very differently if it weren't for my walk by grace from then until now. It's had everything to do with the four blocks...and with the moving beyond them.

~

And how, exactly, does what's planted in us from childhood keep us moving through life? I remember a Thanksgiving when I was working in one of the high schools. We were delivering prepared food to families who needed a hot meal. I was driving my BMW in neighborhoods some would have called marginal, if not downright scary. But since my life started within the four blocks of our project, I could talk to anybody. I could connect across class, income, color, all of it.

And how clearly I remember the joy of mothers, aunts and grandmothers greeting the bounty we carried with "Oh, my God!" At each doorstep, I made sure they knew that the food came from their children's school, from their own community, not from some faceless corporate charity far removed from their lives.

"These boys you see delivering baskets are from the school. We're here to help. We just want everyone to have a hot meal."

One of the mothers said, "We were just praying. We didn't know where it might come from."

"Well here you go," I said, "Here's a nice Thanksgiving meal. God answers prayers."

In the newsletter the school published, I emphasized that our Thanksgiving delivery came from the community. I didn't want anyone to think that what we were doing was a case of "us and them". They needed to know it was all just "us." A few days after the holiday, some of the boys who had helped deliver the baskets caught me in the hall to say, "Ms. Cernata, you don't know what you've done."

~

Another goal, formulated in my later years, is to leave a legacy with my kids that inspires them to multiply the heritage that nurtured me through my childhood in The Berg; a legacy that moves them and that heritage beyond what they know right now. I pray they may be thankful for all those long-ago families who lived in our four blocks, the ones who taught me that the world is big enough for all of us.

EPILOGUE

*"Comfort food? Why, that's greens,
preferably turnips, fresh-baked rolls
and the chicken your mother just fried."*

~ Dr.C

1.
AM I STILL CERNATA THE WARRIOR?

These days, I hold my precious memories closer, because they sustain me. Much else gets tossed. I choose to be around people who light me up. Anyone else, while they're being forgiven, is invited to stay back; No need to step over my threshold. Collecting my precious memories into the new mosaic of my life allows me to forgive myself, as I forgive others, to step out, to walk on. Just recently, my sister and I went to worship at her new church. I witnessed the congregation welcome her, extending "the right hand of fellowship."

Asking if I'm still The Warrior, I pray that I carry light instead of its opposite. Let me be an Enlightened Warrior destined to help others find a way to lift their voices.

2.
MRS. AYERS

My mom's funeral was standing room only.

Do you remember Mrs. Ayers, who so loved my mother, and treated our family with great kindness? It seems that she did not forget us. I remember seeing Mrs. Ayers walk by my mother's coffin and break down weeping. She adored my mom. Ms. Ayers also came to my wedding. There's a picture of her holding me gently, looking at me fondly. And she's saying, "Catherine would be so proud of you. You look so much like her. You've grown up to be such a beautiful girl."

3.
THE PRESSING COMB

I still have my mother's pressing comb.

It's old, but suitable for framing. I think that's what I want to do with it. Framed, it can hang on the wall, and I know just the spot where it will catch my glance every time I walk by. I'll look at it and remember…

Us, sitting around one small table for Sunday dinner. My mother serving my father the chicken breast, his favorite piece. After her mother and the kids are served, my mother makes her own plate from what was left—the back. This echoes in me. How can it not? I now have the option to walk into any 5-star restaurant and place my order for a prime cut of meat, cooked just so. My mother never had that choice, but she paved the way for me to choose.

Yet, when I do, I'm unable to keep from remembering …

4

THAT NAME

Zierre and I have a reservation for lunch.

It's Christmas of President Obama's last year in office, and we had just finished a tour of the White House. As my grandson and I walked up F Street in D. C., toward the restaurant holding our reservation, we noticed the old name still inscribed in stone on the building. Going through the beautiful revolving door that now marks the entrance to The Hamilton Restaurant, it hit me. What was once the back door is now the front door.

Silently, I speak to my mother's spirit: "Mom, we've broken this barrier. We're in here. We're walking right through the same entrance. I'm taking your great-grandson into a place where, once, we were not welcome." In memory I see my father standing outside Garfinkel's old back door, the one reserved *for colored only.* He's fuming as my mother works inside, quickly sketching. I get chills.

"And, Mama, we have a reservation under the name: Dr. Morse."

But, of course, since its holiday season, Hamilton's is crowded and overbooked. Shuffling slowly through the long line with, "Nana, I'm hungry," coming from Zierre, it seems practical to seek a less in-demand place to feed my grandson. But surely it was intended that we share this experience. As we walk out of the department store-turned-restaurant, we look again at the engraving on the side of the building. *That name*...Garfinckel's.

"Zierre, let me tell you a story," I begin. He absorbs what he's told...that's one of his gifts. When I finish, I hear, "I'm proud of you, Nana." I say, "I think she would be proud of you, too. Now, let's go get that hamburger!"

When I'd spoken to the manager to cancel our reservation, he offered his card as a raincheck for dinner on him "anytime you want to come back." I did go back for that dinner, with one of my daughters, and one of my mentors.

5.
LETTERS

I found them in a box after we moved to the new house.

All of Roger's letters addressed from his school, Missouri State, to our home on Oronoco Street, were in a box in the garage. In the letters, one for every day, he pours out his love to his pregnant wife, my sister Val, and his first-born daughter. Also in the box are letters to "Mama Catherine." In these, his gratitude is obvious; he thanks his mother-in-law for caring for his children so that he and my sister can get their educations and still have a family. His respect and affection for "Mama Catherine" fills up every line: "I will forever be indebted." Long afterwards, after divorce and the death of my sister's second husband, Roger returned to us. Briefly, we were a family again. My sister has also retrieved some letters from the box and re-read the ones to her. Perhaps the tenderness is too much to bear, because after a while she sets them aside until the day when she can welcome such emotions back into her life. For the moment, she moves forward with humility and a willingness to be in open dialogue with us all.

6.
I SEEM TO HAVE BECOME THE FAMILY MATRIARCH

During my sister's years of hardship, far from taking on the responsibilities of a matriarch, she could barely care for herself. At some point, long forgotten, I realized I had inherited the role. Someone needed to fill in the gaps as a mother to her daughters, and be that woman who got things done. Our family has always honored our matriarchs. You, who may take on that role, will know this truth: to be a matriarch you have to be ready for anything, dishing out practical advice and comfort by the armful. My sister complained a bit about the reversal of roles, only to take it back when I explained I didn't want to replace her as a mother. It was, simply, *circumstances* that drove us there.

Val and I are making up for lost time. When she mentioned that she'd like to go see a performance of "The Birth of Christ" in Pennsylvania, but that getting there seemed unlikely, I made sure she could go. The more you give to others, the more God gives to you.

That's all I know.

7.
DUET

My sister is an alto, I am a soprano. We are planning to sing a duet, which seems right. It's time to come full circle and join voices. I've made it very clear to the pastor in her new church that he must never underestimate my sister and her talent. And when she needs someone to pitch in to sing "The Blood of Jesus," as soprano to her alto, I'll put on my robes. I'm motivated by the memory of a time, some while ago, when Denyce Graves stepped up with a special invitation for me to come as her guest to a Christmas Concert at the National Cathedral where she would be performing. As the big car sped along the streets from PBS on Braddock Street to the destination in D.C., I had to remember…Ms. Graves believed I had a voice to sing.

Therefore, I will sing.

8.
GOD'S IMPECCABLE TIMING

I hear her, the genre-busting queen of song…
Aretha Franklin. The sound comes from my sister's 45s, played on a Saturday, back home in The Berg. It's the song of Moses leading his people across the waters to a New Jerusalem. Written in first person singular, "How I Got Over" is the ultimate psalm of gratitude. You better listen to it right now. Then you'll know how I got over.

Thank you, God. As promised, you have watched over my comings and goings.

Your timing is impeccable.

- 0 -

ACKNOWLEDGEMENTS

Acknowledging those who have impacted my life would take a life-time. I hardly know where to begin. I'm grateful for my upbringing that taught me the true meaning of God, love, and family. The Four Blocks built the foundation of my life. I honor my Grandmother and Parents, you will forever be embedded in my heart—until we meet again! To my Sister, despite our challenging times, thanks for your "final act of love and forgiveness!" Thanks for loving me just as I am. To my beautiful nieces, I love you beyond measure. You've been an integral part of my life every step of my journey. I couldn't imagine my life without the two of you!

To my Morse Crew—"Triple Threat", Zack II, Znada, and Zelexis: I would not be the person I am without the three of you. I love you beyond your wildest imagination. I grew up with you and learned the true meaning of loving unconditionally. Thank you for loving me as momma through ALL of my faults. Thank you for never giving up on me; you're my biggest champions in pursuit of my destiny.

To my grandchildren—Zierre, Yareli, Caleb, Baylie Grey, and Zorian: my Morse Crew Plus Five. My goal is to leave you and future generations a legacy of knowing you're "planted with a purpose" in life!

To my mentor Dr. Henry Johnson—thank you for the opportunity and challenge to become a better Cernata! To my colleague and friend Dr. Michael Wood—thank you for that hard conversation one evening while working the basketball game at West Potomac High. You made it clear: the time to change was now! Look at the outcome! I love you Dr. Mike.

To my lifelong mentor and friend Dr. Walter "Ray" McCollum: No words can express my heartfelt gratitude and appreciation for how you've impacted my life. You saw the potential in me that I didn't see in myself. You've created the opportunity and prepared me to become a scholar/practitioner. I'm on my academic journey impacting students' lives beyond my imagination. My goal for my kids, grandchildren, family, and friends is to leave a legacy emphasizing the power of determination, sacrifice, and commitment; to use every obstacle as an opportunity to the next step in success.

I'm grateful that God has placed a very special someone in my life who loves me for being me. It hasn't been easy, though rewarding I believe, for him to witness my progress from a "bed of dying" to walking in my purpose. I'm grateful to be loved! One Love, Tony.

And, of course, I owe everything to God's impeccable timing. He has destined and orchestrated everything about my life. I've prevailed and awakened to discover what it means to be "living my best life!

Finally, I must praise my dear readers. You've traveled the road with me through a journey of many twists and turns. But as I contemplate all that's happening now and what may be next, I must acknowledge the ones who helped get me here.

For helping me fulfill the dream of higher education and the chance to be a professor in a career I love, I must thank my mentors, who even now are pushing me on to the next step. Perhaps a university dean, even a provost?

I love the ability to teach, coach, and mentor, and wish to acknowledge all those students who have inspired me to continue and build on that career while reaching out to my peers to gain a reputation as a scholar/practitioner.

I must also thank my adult learners. You are the folks who arrive with the same fears I had walking into that classroom in 2004. But wow! Now I have entrepreneurs in my class! I salute you.

I'm grateful to my clients in the executive leadership sphere, who are willing to look creatively at new ways to advance their cause or their business. A place where I'm always glad to help them go.

I am grateful to the Nesbitts, Brenda and Alec, who have guided me on the road to becoming an author, one whose books, I hope, will make a difference in people's lives. A special tribute to Brenda Nesbitt for our year long journey of coaching and writing.

And to my dear friend and spiritual advisor Bishop Erwin A. Scofield, who entered my life just when I needed it most. You've been the wise counsel and confidant who always reminded me I was "planted" with a "purpose" to share my testimony with the world. Our friendship will stand the test of time, as you are family.